HANG [barcode] W9-BGQ-536

a vegetarian shrine in an[...]

12East 32nd Street, New York, NY 10016
Tel : 212 213 0077
info@hangawirestaurant.com
www.hangawirestaurant.com

https://www.facebook.com/hangawinyc

http://twitter.com/hangawinyc

HANGAWI

The

Vegan Guide

To

New York City

RYNN BERRY & CHRIS A. SUZUKI

With Barry Litsky, J.D.

Published by

Ethical Living

This book is dedicated to FM Esfandiary, Napoleao Nelson Salgado-Santos, and to all people who respect animals enough not to eat them or consume their byproducts.

•

Twentieth edition, 2014

ISBN 13: 978-0-9788132-8-4
ISBN 10: 0-9788132 8-6

Library of Congress Number 2001-135857

This book is printed on durable, acid-free paper.

Published in the United States by Ethical Living
P O Box 8174
JAF Station
New York, NY 10116

Cover design and title page design by Donna Hughes; Dr. Chris Abreu-Suzuki, and Barbara Berasi. Cover drawing by Sarah Caplan. Copyright © by Rynn Berry and Chris Abreu-Suzuki.

Our thanks to Barbara Berasi, Diane Brandt, and J.C. Oliveira.

Special Thanks to Carolyn Handel.

CONTENTS

Appreciations

"More than a food guide, a portable conscience. "

New York Times

"The Vegan Guide to New York City is a very complete Guide!"

The New York Daily News

"Packed with information and insightful commentary, THE VEGAN GUIDE TO NEW YORK CITY invites you to take a juicy, cholesterol-free, cruelty-free bite out of the Big Apple.

Michael Klaper, M.D.
Author, Vegan Nutrition: Pure and Simple

"Indispensable for the traveling vegan, this guide will most definitely enhance the vegan experience in New York. As a long-time resident of this city, I learned a great deal!"

Gary Francione, Professor of Law, Rutgers University
Director, Animal Rights Law Clinic

"Also, order a copy of the book, *The Vegan Guide to New York City*, and don't forget to pack it with you on your trip (along with this post)!"
PETA PRIME TRAVELER

NYC Vegan Fitness Vacations

WWW.NYCVEGFITNESSVACATIONS.COM

3 DAY WEEKEND GETAWAYS!

- Fine dining
- Broadway shows
- Sightseeing
- Fitness training
- Massage therapy
- Vegan shoe shopping
- All expenses included!

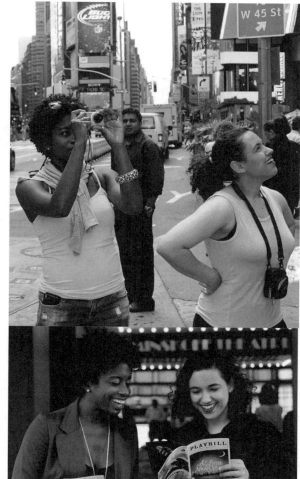

/ l \

A WORD FROM THE AUTHORS

We love food. Whatever image the uninformed may hold of vegans as joyless ascetics who subsist on carrots and brown rice, it certainly does not hold true for us. We love to eat from a world of varied cuisines—a simple macrobiotic meal of miso soup and steamed vegetables one day, a sumptuous Italian feast of grilled pizza with roasted sweet peppers and portobello mushrooms the next, a rich Thai or Indian curry dinner the third—and one of the joys of New York City is that you can find them all within the same block. That's because New York is a world city.

The Vegan Guide to New York City was launched back in 1994, when Rynn Berry, Max Friedman, and Dan Mills, under the tutelage of Alex Bourke, author of Vegetarian London, put together the first slender edition. That same year Dan went back to London to practice law, and Max went to graduate school to get a Ph.D. in American History. That left Rynn Berry in New York City to carry on with the Vegan Guide. In the years since, Rynn has put out a new edition of the guide annually. In 2001, he joined forces with Chris Abreu Suzuki, and Barry Litsky to put out the first quality paperback edition of the Vegan Guide. Rynn, Chris and Barry met at the Farm Sanctuary, a refuge for farm animals in Watkins Glen, New York.

Rynn Berry is the historical advisor to the North American Vegetarian Society. He is the author of several seminal books on vegetarianism; they include The New Vegetarians, Famous Vegetarians and Their Favorite Recipes, Hitler: Neither Vegetarian Nor Animal Lover, and Food for The Gods Vegetarianism and the World's Religions. In 2004, Rynn was commissioned to write a 6,000 word entry on the history of vegetarianism in the US for the Oxford Encyclopedia of Food and Drink in America. In 2010 Rynn co-authored the book, *Becoming Raw*. Rynn contributes frequently to both scholarly and spiritual publications.

Chris Abreu-Suzuki, Ph.D., is a professor of Mathematics, a long distance runner, who has won many races, a fervent animal rights activist and a connoisseur of vegan food. She's been a vegan since 1992 and an ethical vegetarian since 1977.

Barry Litsky, an intellectual property lawyer, who lives in New York City, does pro bono work for animal rights causes. He is also a vegetarian gourmet, who loves to whip up vegan meals for friends in his apartment.

A FEW NOTES ON DINING IN NEW YORK...

There are more than 100 restaurants described in this book, but by no means should you limit yourself to them. New York is a city where you have the wide world at your doorstep, and you should not hesitate to plunge right in. All the restaurants listed in this guide offer vegan meals, but vegans will also do well at restaurants that do not go out of their way to cater to them, bearing in mind a few basic principles.

There are two centers for Indian food in town. One is 6th Street between 1st and 2nd Avenues, a block known as "Little India" for its cheek-by-jowl Indian restaurants. The joke is that there's one kitchen and a conveyor belt. Less well known to tourists is the community on Lexington around 28th Street, where the patrons are often Indian, too. As a rule, you should ask if they cook with ghee (clarified butter). We've listed Indian restaurants that use oil in most of their dishes, but ask anyway. You can request that they leave off the raita (yogurt with cucumbers).

There has been a boom in the popularity of Mexican food in the United States in the past few years, notably when salsa bypassed ketchup in condiment sales. In Mexico, Mexican food is based on corn or wheat with beans, but prepared with lard, cheese and meat stock, making strict vegan travel there a challenge. In New York City, there are a few authentic and many cheap Americanized places to eat Mexican food unsuitable for vegans. However, the last five years has seen an explosion in the number of trendy, "Cal-Mex" or "Tex-Mex" or "San Francisco Style" restaurants serving a healthy variation of Mexican cuisine prepared without lard, containing fresh vegetables and usually with the option of soy cheese, whole wheat tortillas and brown rice. (Almost all soy cheeses contain casein, a milk derivative; most tofu sour cream does not. See Glossary.) We have included addresses for these chains of healthy, vegan-friendly Mexican restaurants, where some of the best meals in the city are to be had. While they are similar, we give Burritoville a slight edge over the others:

Some of the most talented chefs in town are at moderate to expensive Italian restaurants. Vegans can always find something to eat here, if you request that your food be prepared with olive oil instead of butter, and make sure they leave out the common flavorings of Parmesan cheese and prosciutto (ham). Fresh pasta is often, but not always, made with egg. At Thai restaurants, it's dried shrimp and fish sauce you want to look out for. But we should offer this caveat: Since non-veg restaurants use utensils and working surfaces that may have come in contact with animal flesh, it is always preferable to eat in vegetarian/ vegan restaurants to avoid cross-contamination. Now go ahead and explore.

Nearly every restaurant in this guide offers take-out (meals to take home) and almost all of them also will deliver food right to your door, if you're in the area (say, within fifteen to twenty blocks). Because this service is nearly universal, we have specified only when a restaurant does NOT deliver or serve take-out. Otherwise, if the weather's bad or you'd rather stay indoors, you can call any one of these places and have your dinner in the comfort of your own room. Delivery is almost always free, usually with a minimum total order of $7-12, and you should tip your delivery person 15% of the bill. You can simply call up and tell them what you want, or ask what they have without meat or milk products; or, better still, do as New Yorkers do and start

your own collection of take-out menus from your favorite restaurants .

Most health food shops offer an assortment of ready-to-eat foods for vegans—hummus sandwiches, nutburgers and salads—in the refrigerator case. These tend to be OK, range in price from two to four dollars and can be just the thing if you want a quick snack. We've made a note by health food shops that go a little further, with a fresh salad bar, sandwich counter or buffet.

More and more liquor stores in New York stock organic wines, and of these, several labels are vegan—they use no fish or eggs in the "fining" (clarifying) process. Look for anything by the Organic Wine Works label or anything by Frey except the 1991 Cabernet, which was fined with egg whites. If you can't find them anywhere, try Warehouse Wines and Spirits at 735 Broadway (at Astor Place) or the slightly more expensive Astor Wines and Spirits at Lafayette and Astor.

An important note for our foreign readers: tax and tip are NOT included in the price at American restaurants, so figure on adding another 8.65% for the city and 15 20% for the service. American servers get paid an abysmal hourly wage and earn most of their salary from tips, so this is not really optional: unless you get terrible service, everyone leaves 15% as a matter of routine, and it's nicer to leave 20%. An exception is when there is no server, as in buffets or self serve cafeterias; and when you dine in a group of more than five persons, the tip ("gratuity") may be figured into your total. People who deliver take-out to your door should also get a 15% tip.

A valid current Student I.D. will get you 10-15% off at many restaurants and some shops. The restaurants are grouped by neighborhood, and listed alphabetically within each neighborhood.

A NOTE ON OUR POLICY OF RESTAURANT SELECTION:

In 1994, when we first launched this guide, the number of vegan and vegetarian restaurants were rather sparse; so we included some vegetarian friendly restaurants that served some meat, but went out of their way to accommodate vegetarians. As of 1996, it was our feeling that we should no longer include any restaurants that served animal flesh of any kind--be it fish or fowl, snail or cow--because all restaurants have become friendlier to vegetarians; so to continue to feature vegetarian friendly restaurants in the Guide would make it meaningless. The vegetarian friendly restaurants that were included in the original guide were grandfathered in and phased out as they closed. In a few instances, restaurants started out as being vegan, then started serving increasing amounts of meat. These were so egregiously non-veg. that we had to delete them from the guide. But from then on, only vegetarian and vegan restaurants were to be included. That's why you may not find the trendy almost-vegetarian restaurant that you've been hearing about. Look to the conventional guides for those. Furthermore, in rating and ranking restaurants, we add and subtract points depending on how vegan they are. In other words, if they use honey or dairy products in their dishes, they will be penalized for it.

THE RESTAURANTS

ve=vegan
v=fleshless with vegan options
AE=American Express
MC=Mastercard
V=Visa
D=Discover

$
$$
$$$

Full service means waiters take your order and bring your food. Counter service means you order at the counter and carry your meal to your table (these are usually cheaper, more casual places, often with paper plates). Prices listed are for typical vegan entrees. Address is listed opposite restaurant name. Nearest cross-streets are under address for easy location.

indicates an inexpesive entree

indicates a moderately priced entree

indicates an expensive entree

HARLEM
(North of Central Park)

UPTOWN VEG. JUICE BAR[v] **$**

Counter service
West Indian
No cards
No alcohol
www.uptownveg.com

14 East 125th Street
bet. Madison/ Fifth Avenues
212-987-2660
daily 8am-10pm

A cross between a small cafe and a juice bar, Uptown Juice Bar is to be prized as much for its food as for its juices. Along with an array of juice combinations and smoothies, it serves delicious Caribbean-style vegan food. And although the menu contains alarming words like beef and fish, these are to be understood as "mock beef" and "mock fish." For instance there is a "turkey" salad, a "chicken" salad and a "fish" salad, but no turkey, chicken or fish died to produce these dishes. They're entirely ersatz and are very tasty. We had one of their combination meals that consisted of collard greens, tofu with black mushrooms, and a vegan shepherd's pie. To wash down this delectable grub, have one of their fruit smoothies or a juice tonic that is designed to cure whatever ails you. For impotence, drink a potent brew of carrot, parsley, cucumber, orange, and papaya juices. For asthma, gulp down a beverage containing carrot, celery, and grapefruit juice. Of course, if you're a vegan of long-standing, you probably don't have any of these ailments, so toast your good health--and your good fortune in being a vegan--with a fruit smoothie instead.

UPPER WEST SIDE
(West 59th Street and Above)

AYURVEDA CAFE [v] **$$**

Full service
South Indian
All cards
No alcohol

706 Amsterdam Avenue
at 94th Street
212-932-2400
daily 11:30am-10:30pm

With its mango-hued walls and mottled sky blue ceilings, the Ayurveda Cafe resembles nothing so much as a film set for an early Merchant-Ivory movie, like Shakespeare Wallah or Bombay Talkie. So, it's not surprising to learn that the owner, Tirlok Malik, is a film director, who has parlayed a side interest in Indian cuisine into what seems to my taste buds to be one of the best Indian restaurants in town. Part Ismail Merchant, part Deepak Chopra with the Chopra ascendant, Malik has based his restaurant's dishes on the teachings of one of the four sacred books of Vedic Hinduism, which dates back at least 3,000 years--the Ayurveda (which means "knowledge of life" in Sanskrit.) Essentially, Ayurvedic cuisine tries to combine the six tastes, sweet. sour, salty, astringent, bitter and pungent, in order to produce a cuisine that is properly balanced for your body type. It certainly was right for my olfactory type. The Thali that I tasted was lightly spiced and lightly cooked so that you could taste each vegetable. I had to skip the raitas and desserts because they all contained dairy products and /or honey. Otherwise, a vegan can dine very handsomely here.

BLOSSOM DU JOUR UPPER WEST [ve] **$$** 👍

165 Amsterdam
bet. 67/68 Streets
212-799-9010
daily 8:30am-10pm

Counter service
Organic vegan fast ;food.
V, MC
No alcohol
www. Blossomdujour.com

See Description under Midtown West

👍 Indicates we especially recommend this restaurant for the quality of the food.

NY COALITION FOR
HEALTHY SCHOOL FOOD

CHANGING HOW
SCHOOLS FEED KIDS.

NYCHSF introduces plant-based (vegan) foods and nutrition education in schools.
Our focus is on plant-based entrees.
We reach 500 students every week with our Food UnEarthed:
Uncovering the Truth About Food Curriculum – let us know if you are interested in
an internship opportunity. Check out our Wellness Wakeup Call program –
nutrition education that takes 30 seconds a day or less.
**WE ARE RESPONSIBLE FOR THE FIRST TWO PUBLIC (non-charter)
VEGETARIAN SCHOOLS IN THE COUNTRY!**

Attend our amazing fall gala in October with tastings
from over 25 vegan restaurants and caterers
– a vegan foodie's dream come true!

**Wouldn't it be great if every school had healthy vegan food on the
menu, and education to help students learn why it's so important?**
Our schools already do – but there are so many more waiting for our help.
Help make the dream come true!
Become a corporate or individual supporter.

healthy**school**food.org

HealthySchoolFood   **914.630.0199**   CoolSchoolFood

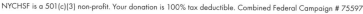

BLOSSOM UPTOWN CAFÉ [ve] $$$ 👍

Full Service
Global vegan, orgainc
All cards
Orgainc beer & wine
www.blossomnyc.com

466 Columbus Avenue
bet. 82nd/ 83rd Streets
212-875-2600
daily 11:30am-10:30pm

See description under Midtown West

CAFE VIVA [A.K.A. VIVA HERBAL PIZZERIA [v] $

Counter service
Italian vegetarian, kosher
All cards
No alcohol

2578 Broadway
bet.97th//98th Streets
212-663-8482
daily 11am-11pm

The founder, Tony Iracani, tells us that Cafe Viva is the only Italian vegetarian restaurant in the US, which after sampling the vegetarian antipasto and the tasty cheeseless pizzas, strikes us as shameful. Italian restaurateurs should beat a path to Cafe Viva to see how vegan Italian food is done, then go forth and do likewise. We had the Pizza Pura, a dairy-free, yeast-free spelt crust, topped with tofu marinated in Miso, grilled veggies and spinach with a vegetarian antipasto on the side. The fridge is stocked with healthful sodas such as Twisted Bean Vanilla Brew, Borealis Birch Beer, Ginseng tonics and China Cola. Recently Cafe Viva has expanded its menu to include a super anti-oxidant pizza; a Zen pizza, which features a green-tea herbal crust; tofu marinated with herbs, and a green tea pesto; it is topped off with a layer of maitake and shitake mushrooms. Another favorite is the Santa Rosa, which consists of a whole wheat crust layered with tofu marinated in miso, and topped off with sun-dried tomatoes and roasted garlic. Viva offers two types of vegan Lasagna as well as vegan Calzones made from spelt and whole wheat. Other pastas such as Raviolis, Strombolis, and Zitis are made from scratch and can be veganized to order. The service staff is friendly and helpful without being obsequious. One of the great pleasures apart from the food is that one can sit and read a paper or chat with a companion for hours without being hurried or pressured. We say, "Viva! Cafe Viva!"

CANDLE CAFE WEST [ve] $$ 👍

Full service
Vegan, organic
All cards
Organic wine, beer, and spirits

2427 broadway
bet. 89th/900th Streets
212-769-8900 & 796-8908 (fax_
M-Sa 11:30am-10:30pm
Su 11:30am-9:30pm

Special gluten-free and kid's menus are available. Available to cater and for private parties and they deliver.

The newest addition to the Candle family, Candle Cafe West, opened to the delight of Upper Westsiders in April 2012. Bart, the founder of Candle Cafe, and his partner, Joy Pierson, have been hounded for years by denizens of the neighborhood to bring their special brand of vegan, organic cuisine West and they are excited to have finally been able to fulfill that wish. The new restaurant is spacious and airy with great light, comfortable seating, and the friendly, passionate, and knowledgeable staff that Candle is known for. Candle Fans will be delighted to find menu staples from Bart and Joy's two East Side locations at the West Side location along with some unique menu items that make Candle Cafe West a destination of its own. In addition to amazing vegan, organic food, Candle Cafe West offers a unique Eco-Bar which serves up an array of outstanding sustainable cocktails, spirits, wines and beers. Selected and crafted by a talented staff of mixoligists and wine connoisseurs, the selection and mix of libations are guaranteed to enhance every visit to Candle Cafe West.

Also look for Candle Cafe Frozen Entrees at Whole Foods Market nationwide, and the Candle Cafe Cookbook and Candle 79 Cookbook, wherever books are sold.

DOABA DELI [v] $

Counter service
Punjabi homestyle
Cash only
No alcohol

945 Columbus Avenue
bet. 106th/ 107th Streets
212-222-2636
daily 6am-5am

"East where the cabbies eat!" is a good ruled of thumb for finding cheap and delicious vegetarian Indian eats. When we noticed clusters of turbaned cabbies idling outside Doaba Deli, we ventured inside, and found a vegetarian Indian chef dishing up the fiery Punjabi cuisine that propels so many Indian cabbies. Although the food is awash in caseous matter, and although the dishes that are vegan are not labeled as such, the vegan fare is hearty and tickles the palate on the way down. It is however necessary to pick one's way gingerly. Never eat anything that contains paneer, (Indian cream cheese, or to be precise: fried, curdled mammary secretions). Tell the chef to make sure your food is cooked in oil rather than ghee (clarified butter). We enjoyed the Aloo Gobi, and the Chana Masala. Doubtless you will too, if you're not a finicky vegan like us.

HUMMUS PLACE/ V [v] $

Full Service
Israeli vegetarian, kosher

2608 Broadway
bet. 98th/99th Streets
212-222-5462

HUMMUS PLACE III [v] $

Full Service
Kosher Israeli hummus house

305 Amstardam Avenue
bet. W. 74th/ W. 75th Streets
212-799-3335

All cards
Wine & Beer

M-Su 10am-12am

See description under Greenwich Village, and other location under East Village, and Upper West Side.

MAOZ II [v] **$**

Counter service
Israeli falafel shack, kosher
All Cards
No alcohol
www.maozusa.com

2047 A Broadway
bet. 70th/ 71st Streets
212-362-2622
daily 11am-12am

See description under Midtown East and other locations under Midtown West, and East Village.

ORGANIC AVENUE [ve] **$$**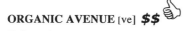

Full service
Organic raw food boutiaue
All major cards
No alcohol
www.organicavenue.com

451 Amsterdam Avenue
at 82nd Street
212-358-0500
M-F 7am-9pm
Sa-Su 9am-9pm

PEACEFOOD CAFÉ [ve] **$$**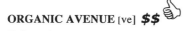

Full service
Vegan world cuisine
All cards
No alcohol
www.peaceefoodcafe.com

460 Amsterdam Avenue
@ 82nd Street
212-362-2266
M-F 10am-10pm
Sa, Su 8am-11pm

We first met Eric when he was training to be a chef at the late-lamented vegetarian restaurant, Urban Spring, in Fort Green, Brooklyn. It was in the winter of '09 and Eric told us that he planned to sell his wildly successful antiques business in Soho and open a vegan restaurant to promote world peace. Eating vegan food, Eric opined with missionary zeal, is conducive to world peace. [Hence the name of his café—PeaceFood.] To be candid, it struck us, at the time, as being a mite quixotic, not to say hopelessly naive. But here we are, four years later --seated at tables in Eric's spiffy Peacefood Café. It is tastefully decorated with a scattering of antiques-- like the Victorian bakery display case that now doubles as a bookcase for vegan books—from Eric's old store. Not only is the food impeccably ethical and vegan, but it is also superbly prepared.

A disciple of the Supreme Master Ching Hai (an amalgam of Christianity and Buddhism founded by former Vietnamese nun, Suma Ching Hai), Eric and his partner, Peter, adhere to the first precept of Buddhism:, which is *ahimsa* [non-violence to all living creatures]. Eric has even gone to the length of inventing a cashew-based vegan substitute for the Roasted Japanese Pumpkin Sandwich. (The roasted pumpkin is mashed with a little sea salt, ground black pepper, and extra virgin olive oil, topped with caramelized onions, ground walnuts, vegan goat cheese, and seasonal greens.) He imported this sandwich--which was originally made with goat cheese-- from the menu of his former employer, the aforementioned, now defunct, Urban Spring.

To special clients, Eric serves what may be described as-- without hyperbole--the best un-cheese burger on the planer. The burger is made from soy and gluten-free wheat, surrounded with melted daiya vegan cheese and jalapeno pepper. Served on two slices of homemade foccacio, it is filled with greens, tomatoes, caramelized onions, and seasoned with a chipotle mustard, vinaigrette sauce. A note of caution: It's so messy, and delicious that it must be eaten with multiple napkins firmly in hand.

The food critics are also lavish in their praise of Eric's dishes. A recent glowing review in the New York Times especially praised Peacefood's Shanghai-style dumplings, which are filled with Chinese chives, shitake and wood ear mushrroms, marianated tofu, and Time Out magazine awarded best chick-pea dish of the year to Peacefood's Chick-Pea Fries.

We started with the The Other Caesar (crisp romaine lettuce, tomatoes, smoked tempeh, red onions and crostini). It was so yummy that we instantly nominated it as best vegan salad of the year! [See Best Vegan Bites.] The Asian Greens (seasonal baby Asian vegetables, nixed sprouts, shredded carrots, tomatoes, marinated and baked tempeh, ground peanuts in a garlic, ginger, ponsu, and sesame dressing)--was a close runner up.

With my partner, Chris, I split a Pan-Seared French Horn Mushrooms Panini. Chris had to restrain me from nominating it as best sandwich of the year, as she felt we were showering Peacefood with too many accolades. Last year's best sandwich of the year is on the menu, as Eric also imported it from Urban Spring.

We tried the new raw dishes: the Raw Lasagna (zucchini, mushrooms, walnut cheese, spinach-basil mix, and tomato sauce), and the Raw Sushi Roll (walnut paste, and seasonal julienned vegetables sushi roll, served with a jicama-carrot medley, topped with avocado). These dishes can stand comparison with those of the best raw food emporia in town, except that the portion sizes at Peacefood are notably generous, yet modestly priced.

The beverages at Peacefood are also superlative. We accompanied our meal with Passionfruit Smoothies, followed by Bombay Delights (coconut, banana, dates, cardamom, nut milk).

Next we supped on pizzas—Roasted Potatoes Pizza (with sautéed mushrooms, oil-cured black olives, and truffle oil); and Mushroom Duxelle Pizza (with roasted sweet peppers, onions. and zucchini). This time we could not but concur--the mushroom pizza was absolutely tip-top. So in our Best Vegan Bites section, you'll find it listed as best pizza of the year.

For dessert we reveled in the raw Key-Lime Pie, and Eric's favorite sweet, the Cinnamon Bun, which we followed with soy cappuccino sweetened with agave nectar. It was the prefect coda to a peace-promoting meal, putting us in mind of a variant on a lyric from a John Lennon song—"All we are saying is give Peacefood a chance."

SARAVANA BHAVANA-UPPER WEST SIDE (v) $

	431 Amsterdam Avenue
Full service	bet 79th/80th Streets
Chennai homestyle	(212) 721-7755
(major cards)	Lunch Tu-Su 12m-4pm
Wine & beer	Dinner 5:30pm-10pm

http://www.saravanaabhavannyc.com
See description under Midtown East.

SOOMSOOM) [v] $

	533 West 72ng Street
Counter service	bet Amsterdam' Columbus
Israeli falafel shack	212-712-2525
All cards	Su-Th 10am-11pm: F 10am-7pm
No alcohol	
www.mysoomsoom.com	

It looks as though the vegetarian falafel shack may soon displace the hamburger hut as New York City's fast food joint of choice. [To that eventuality, we say, in the immortal words of

Ali Baba, "Open sesame!"] Soomsoom, which means "sesame" in Hebrew, is the newest manifestation of this trend.

The falafel balls here are bursting with flavor; they have a crisp brown jacket that conceals a moist, green chickpea and cilantro mixture. By the bright, bubbly ladies who work behind the counter—(one of whom was a vegan)--falafels were stuffed into a pita pocket that was artfully sauced with tahini. We then took our pita pockets to the salad bar and crammed them with chopped cucumbers, chopped tomatoes, a vegan cabbage slaw, and sealed them with a diabolic hot sauce. My friend had a side order of Sweet Potato Fries, which set off the Falafel sandwich quite nicely.

Vegans will of course eschew the Shakshuka Plate (a tomato stew of which the egg is an ineradicable ingredient;) the Sabich (a huumus and eggplant sandwich that may be ordered without the egg).

Perched precariously on stools in front of Soomsoom's storefront window—[All the other seats were taken.]--we sipped a mint lemonade. Then we gazed at the passersby as we savored our falafel sandwiches, trying to protract the taste sensation as long as possible.

Indicates we especially recommend this restaurant for the quality of the food.

CANDLE CAFE [ve] $$$ 👍

Full service
Vegan, organic
All cards
Organic wine and beer
www. candlecafe.com

307 Third Avenue
bet. 74th/75th Streets
12-472-0970 & 472-7169(fax)
M-Sa 11:30am-10:30pm
Su 11:30am-9:30pm

Special gluten-free and kid's menus are available. Delivery, Take-Out and Catering available

Back in the days when Bart Potenza, Candle's tousle-haired founder, ran a juice bar called the Healthy Candle, he dreamed of owning a vegan restaurant. A few years later, he realized his dream when he opened Candle Cafe. *Nineteen* years later, Candle Cafe has metamorphosed into one of New York's most popular eateries where celebrity watchers can spot environmental- and health-conscious actors like Woody Harrelson, and Alicia Silverstone, or prominent Animal Rights activists like Eddy Lama of The Witness , or Harold Brown of The Peaceable Kingdom.

They come here because Bart and his partner, Joy Pierson, have a history of supporting environmental and animal rights causes and because they serve up some of the tastiest vegan food in town. We found just about everything on the menu appetizing, but our particular favorites were as follows: Our favorite appetizer was the Seitan Chimichurri (South American marinated seitan skewers with creamy *citrus-herb* sauce.) Our favorite entree was the *Sesame Crusted Tofu, served with black rice pilaf, steamed greens and sauteed gingered vegetables and a green coconut curry sauce.* We also relished the Tuscan Lasagna with saut ê ed green, Tofu-Basil Ricotta, and Seitan Ragout with a Truffled Tomato Sauce. For dessert, we fell upon the Chocolate Mousse Pie and the Decadent Chocolate-Peanut Butter Cafe with Chocolate Frosting. When it comes to Seitan dishes, which are the forte of both Candle Cafe and Candle 79, no other restaurant can hold a candle to the Candles. Also look for Candle Cafe Frozen Entrees at Whole Foods Market nationwide, and the Candle Cafe Cookbook and Candle 79 Cookbook, wherever books are sold.

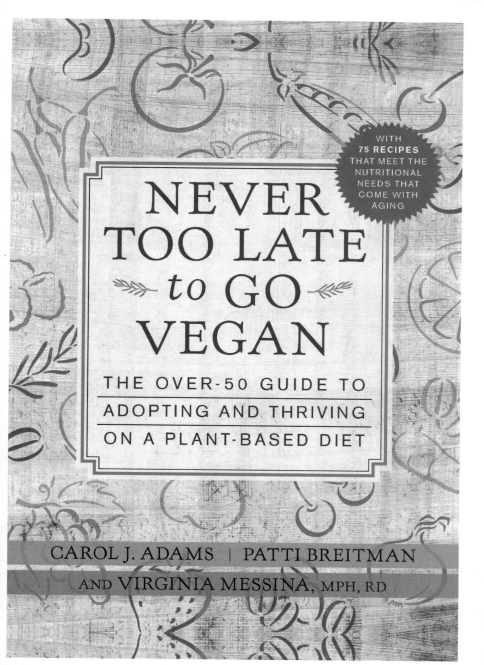

WITH
75 RECIPES
THAT MEET THE
NUTRITIONAL
NEEDS THAT
COME WITH
AGING

NEVER TOO LATE *to* GO VEGAN

THE OVER-50 GUIDE TO
ADOPTING AND THRIVING
ON A PLANT-BASED DIET

CAROL J. ADAMS | PATTI BREITMAN

AND VIRGINIA MESSINA, MPH, RD

CANDLE 79 [ve] **$$$**

Full service
Global organic vegan
All cards
Organic wines, beers and sakes.
www.candle79.com)

154 East 79th Street
at Lexington Avenue
212-537-7179 & 212-472-0860 (fax)
M-F Lunch, 12pm-3:30pm
Dinner, 5:30pm-10:30pm
Sa Brunch 12pm-3:30pm Dinner, 5pm-10pm
Su   Brunch, 12pm-4pm Dinner, 5pm-10pm

A special gluten-free menu is available. Private party rooms and Catering are also available.

New York's Upper East Side has a posh vegan restaurant serving Global Organic style vegan cuisine that can rival --in elegance and excellence- the best restaurants of the world.

Bart Potenza and his partner Joy Pierson have transformed an unprepossessing two-story town house that was formerly a prosaic restaurant called the Dining Room into a restaurant whose interior design is as ravishing as are the dishes on its bill of fare. Start with a glass of organic Sangria at the intimate downstairs wine, sake, and spirits bar. With an extensive all-organic cocktail list, Candle 79's sleek and sexy bar is a popular spot for eco-chic dates!

At the table, begin with the Teaser: delicious Saffron Lobster Mushroom Ravioli, with cashew ricotta, roasted tomato-truffle sauce, spinach, shallots and crispy capers. Then proceed to the Wild Mushroom Salad with Arugula, Grape Tomatoes, Roasted Cippolini Onions, and Creamy Horseradish Dressing. Then on to the main course of Caribbean Jerk Grilled Seitan, with brown ale-black bean sauce, plantains, collard greens, and mango-papaya salsa. If you are a rawfoodist, try the wonderfully flavorful Live Heirloom Tomato-Zucchini Lasagna. Finish with the ever-addictive Chocolate-Peanut Butter Bliss- a creamy mousse confection nestled in a dark chocolate shell. Be sure to check the current menu on-line (www.candle79.com) as it changes with the season according to local organic produce. Much of the credit for Candle 79's dazzling menu is owed to head chef Angel Ramos, and pastry chef Jorge Pineda. We are avid fans of their seitan dishes both at Candle Cafe and at Candle 79. They have raised the preparation of Seitan to high art. Indeed, their Seitan Piccata (Sir Paul McCartney's favorite!)with Creamed Spinach, Savory Potato Cake and Lemon-Caper Sauce should make Seitan worshippers of even the most fundamentalist carnivore. Congratulations   to Candle 79 for being named "Best Vegetarian Restaurant " in Zagat's 2007 and 2008, and for their recent rave New York Times Review, in which Frank Bruni wrote that Candle 79 "showed him the light!"Be sure to look for their latest stunning creation, the Candle 79 Cookbook, available wherever books are sold

GOBO [ve] $$

Full service
Organic, Asian-Western fusion cuisine
All cards
Organic beer & wine
www.goborestaurant.com

1426 Third Avenue
at 81st Street
212-288-4686
Su-We 11:30am-11:30pm
Th-Sa 11:30am-12am

See the description under East Village.

GREEN BEAN CAFE, THE [v] $

Counter service
Homestyle organic vegetarian
Visa & Mastercard
No alcohol
www. BeanGoneGreen.com

1413 York Avenue
bet. 75th/ 76th Streets
212-861-1539
M-F 7am-9pm
Sa, Su 9am-9pm

When we walked into the Green Bean, shortly after it opened, we saw three generations of the owner's family all of whom were vegetarian, all working behind the counter. There's Darrel the owner, Darrel's mother, Barbara, and Darrel's nephew, Nirmal. Darrel also owns the restaurant down the block called Beanochio. In fact, the Green Bean now occupies the space formerly inhabited by Beanocchio, which outgrew its space. That's what beans do; they grow and grow as if by magic.

As we know from *Jack and the Beanstalk,* beans have magical properties. And this Green Bean is no exception. Magical is it that such a small space can produce such a high volume of high quality dishes and beverages. Appropriately enough we started with a beany dish--their Spicy Tempeh with Mixed Greens and Sweet Potatoes. Superb! Next we tried their Seitan Cutlets with Mashed Potatoes and Miso Gravy. Pluperfect!

Their smoothies are made with organic frozen fruit and contain no added ice. (Most juice bars spike their fruit with superadded ice as a stretcher.) We quaffed the Berry Smoothie, and ii really socked our knocks off!

For dessert we munched cookies and cupcakes, which are all vegan, all delicious, and all baked downstairs in the basement. For those who like their desserts unbaked, The Green Bean now offers an array of raw cakes, pies and cookies.[Not to mention raw savories.] We capped off our meal by sharing a scrumptious raw carrot cake. Needless to say, we left feeling satisfied and full of beans, magic beans

JUICE PRESS, THE [v] $$

Counter service
Organic Juices and raw food
All Cards
No alcohol

1050 Third Avenue
at 62nd Street
212-777-0034
daily 8am-8pm

Thejuicepressonline.com

See description under East Village

ORGANIC AVENUE [ve] $$ 👍

Full service
Organic raw food boutiaue
All major cards
No alcohol
www.organicavenue.com

1021 Lexingron Avenue
at bet. 73rd/ 74th Streets
212-358-0500
daily 8am-9pm

PONGAL [v] $$

Full service
Indian vegetarian
All majjor cards
No alcohol
See description under Midtown East.

1154 First Avnue
at 63rd Street
212-355-4600
Th 11:30am-10pm
F-Su 11:30am-10:30pm

PURE FOOD [ve] $$

Counter service
Salad and juice bar
All majjor cards
No alcohol
www.purefood.com

1396 Madison Avenue
at 97th Street
212-996-7500
M-F:7am-8pm
Sa-Su 8am-8pm

Pure Food is not to be confused with its posh namesake, Pure Food and Wine near Gramercy Park. It proudly proclaims its veganism with a large sign in front, shouting VEGAN to the passersby—something that the proprietors of Pure Food & Wine would consider *infra dignitas*. Still one-third of their fare is raw, much of it quite tasty. We relished their quinoa-based vegiburger, and their salad combinations such as kale avocado and tomato. Their green smoothies are not to be missed.

SOFT SERVE FRUIT CO. [v] $

Counter service
Soft serve shack
All cards
No alcohol
www.simplypeeled.com

1371 Third Avenue
bet. 78th/ 79th Streets
212-794-2200
M-Th,Su 7:30am-10:00pm
F,Sa 7:30am-11pm

The four partners who own The Soft Serve Fruit Co., (formerly Simply Peeled), were casting about for a healthy alternative to the malevolent iced glop served at the sleazy frozen yogurt shops and seedy ice-cream parlors that litter the Upper East Side landscape. Using a technique of their own devising, which combines pureed fruit, filtered water, and a hint of organic cane sugar---in their own kitchen, they concocted a sort of frozen sorbet that has the consistency of soft-serve ice-cream. They called it Fruizo.

Fruizo comes in three flavors—mango, banana, and strawberry. We had the Bandango Sundae (banana and mango fruizo, topped with tortilla chips, salsa and chopped mango bits). We also tried the Fruit Salad Sundae (banana, strawberry and mango Fruizo topped with berries, raisins, granola and cheerios.)

To be quite candid, we found the straight Fruizo to be somewhat bland; but when we added the toppings, the Fruizo came to life. There is a choice of 24 different toppings-only a few of which are non-vegan. The non-vegan toppings are the chocolate chips, which are made with milk, and the granola, which is made with honey. Fruizo is also used to make smoothies. We tried the Very Berry in which Fruizo is blended with blueberries, strawberries and raspberries.) This was an appealing treat, but we had to expostulate to the counter person that we didn't want skim milk, or honey, or protein powders added to it. Although we much prefer the vegan ice-cream parlors like Stogo and Lula's Sweet Apothecary that are located in the East Village, there is definitely a place for Fruizo in a neighborhood that is awash in frozen mammary secretion

VEGAN DIVAS [v] $

Counter service
Baked goods and desserts
Visa & Mastercard
No alcohol
www.vegandivasnyc.com

1437 First Avenue
bet. 74th/ 75th Streets
212-734-0845
M-Sa 7:30am-8pm
Su 10am-5pm

Vegan Divas is a new vegan bakery on the upper east side of Manhattan. Its advent is very welcome in this high rent, high cholesterol district. It was founded in the fall of 2012 by Fernanda Capobianca, who is that *rara avis*, a vegan from Brazil, one of the most carnivorous nations on the planet.

When we crossed the threshold to enter the store's elegant interior, we were enchanted to see quotes from our favorite vegans from history (Pythagoras, Leonardo da Vinci, et al.) emblazoned on the main wall. The cakes and doughnuts and pies were displayed in splendid profusion. However, we were less taken with the person behind the counter who seemed unwilling to answer our questions, and rushed us through our order. She wasn't wearing a hair net, or gloves when she handled the food, and we felt she was underdressed and under-motivated for the job.

Undaunted, we ordered a savory quiche, and a zucchini tart, which we had trouble telling apart. The Double Brownie was rather ordinary tasting. The doughnut was satisfactory, but it tasted more like a Bundt cake. What we liked about the raspberry cheesecake was that its jam was intensely flavorful without being over-sugared.. We chased everything with a bracing beverage, a Macchiatto an Espresso coffee made with hot chocolate and soy milk.

We were eager to taste the passion fruit mousse, and the soy yogurt with acai, as both had been touted in the Vogue article about the place, but both were inexplicably unavailable. A daily savory sandwich, which was featured on the menu, was also inexplicably unavailable. At first glance, all the comestibles at Diva looked toothsome, and delicious, but we found that when we sank our teeth into them, they were missing a certain *Je ne sais quois*

.V-NOTE [ve] **$$$**

Full Service
Vegan Bistro & Wine Bar
All cards
Organic beer & wine
www.blossomnyc.com

1522 First Avenue
bet. 79th/ 80th Streets
212-249-5009
daily 11:30am-10:30pm

Just there short blocks away from Candle 79 , which it rivals in quality and service, is The V-Note a new deluxe vegan restaurant on the Upper East Side. It was started by Ronen Seri, the co-founder of Blossom. (In fact it is located on the site of the short-lived Blossom East.) So we were not too surprised to see some cherished items from Blossom show up on the menu.

V-Note is set in a rectangular shaped room with black walls adorned with large, colorful abstract paintings. All the tables were occupied when we arrived, so we were seated at the end of the bar where folks were sipping vintage wines and downing entrees rather than drowning their sorrows with booze. Case in point: We couldn't help noticing that the lady sitting to our left was sipping a Riesling while tucking into a Pasta Bolognese and perusing an article in the New Yorker on her i-pad.

Entirely vegan is the menu, and the wait staff! To a person, each waiter said, all unbidden, that he loved his job; liked working under Ronen; and wouldn't think of working anywhere else. We asked Chris, the headwaiter, to recommend an appetizer; he suggested the Black-Eyed Pea Cake. We were not disappointed. A piquant and flavorful cake composed of Yukon gold potatoes, black-eyed peas, and a chipotle aoli was set before us. We downed it with unseemly gusto.

Since we had done so well by Chris, we asked him to recommend an entrée. Medallions *Au Poivre*, he said unhesitatingly. [Seitan Medallions in a French peppercorn sauce are served with a cauliflauer-poatato puree, and steamed aasparagus.] They're so addictive that headwaiter Chris, who can select anything on the menu *gratis,* dines on them four times a week. We could easily see why. We tossed off the Medallions with a Calypso, a smoothie consisting of raspberry, pineapple, and banana. To be quire frank, most restaurant smoothies are execrable, but this one was worthy of Jill Larsen's Magic Mix Juicery.

Also, on headwaiter Chris' recommendation, we wolfed the Wilted Spinach Salad with its soy bacon crumbles, roasted corn, shitake, tempeh and cashews, dressed with a balsamic vinaigrette.

For dessert, however, we decided to ignore Chris's recommendation of the Chocolate Ganache cake as being too redolent of Blossom, (where it is a cherished item on the dessert menu) in favor of the Tiramasu, topped *a la mode* with a scoop of soy vanilla ice-cream.

We were lucky to have dined at the V-Note on a Friday evening because there is live music on Fridays and Saturdays. An Argentine guitarist of no mean talent melts the house with his sultry licks. With the V-Note, owner Ronen Seri has struck just the right vegan note.

Blossom
Premier Vegan Eateries

Organic Dining in the *Hearts* of NYC

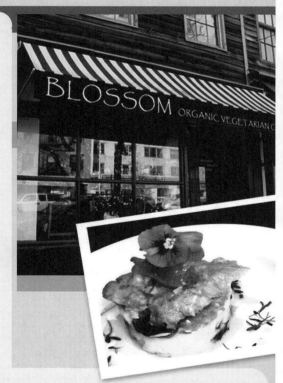

MIDTOWN WEST and Chelsea
(West 14th to West 59th Streets)

BEYOND SUSHI –CHELSEA MARKET [ve] **$**

75 9th Avenue
at 15th Street
212-929-2889
daily 10am-9pm

Counter Service
Vegan kosher sushi
All cards
No alcohol
www. BeyondSushiNYC.Com

See description under East Village

BLOSSOM DINING [ve] **$$$**

187 Ninth Avenue
bet. 21st/ 22nd Streets
212-627-1144
daily 11:30am-10:30pm

Full Service
Global vegan, orgainc
All cards
Organic beer & wine
www.blossomnyc.com

Erstwhile actors, Ronen Seri, and his wife Pamela, couldn't find a restaurant to satisfy their recherché vegan tastes; so they decided to open their own place. We vegan foodies are all in their debt. For now we have someplace to go besides Candle '79, on the upper east side, and Millennium, in San Francisco, to slake our appetite for organic vegan haute cuisine.

Indeed the restaurant's interior has a touch of the theater about it. With its chic townhouse setting; its cozy fireplace; its burnished wood tables; its floor-to-ceiling draperies; it looks like the perfect stage set for a posh restaurant

Despite their restaurant's high-toned elegance, Ronen and Pamela are not above stating, right on their menu, that "Blossom is first and foremost animal caring." Consequently, their "food is not only organic, it is also dairy and cholesterol free." This is the first time we know of that a restaurateur has had the courage to remind his/her patrons that conventional non-veg. food involves the wanton sacrifice of our fellow creatures.

We would eat at Blossom out of solidarity with Ronen and Pamela--just to pay tribute to their ethical approach to food preparation--but, fortunately, their food is so extraordinary that we also eat there for the sheer yumminess of the dishes.

Everyone we know. in our circle of vegan friends , raves about Blossom's appetizers-- especially the South Asian Lumpia (curried seitan and potatoes wrapped in a crispy chickpea crepe, served with mango onion sambal). And, we are here to confirm that it, and the Black-Eyed Pea Cake (crispy cake of yukon gold potato & black-eyed peas, served with chipotle aioli) are as

fresh and peppery as they're cracked up to be.

We're confessed seitan worshippers; so we reveled in the Barbecued Seitan Sandwich (barbecued seitan and caramelized onions with fresh cut fries or salad); and the Seitan Medallions (pan seared seitan cutlets served with herbed soft polenta and broccoli rabe). They would have delighted Old Split-foot himself, [who like most ungulates is doubtless a vegan].

For dessert we had the Chocolate Ganache Cake (a layered combination of rich chocolate ganache and chocolate cake). And the Pineapple Crepe (grilled pineapple wrapped in a crepe served with coconut reduction and green tea or vanilla ice-cream). It was a fitting climax to this play in three courses. We were chagrined--as with most extraordinary theater--only that it had to end.

.BLOSSOM DU JOUR--MIDTOWN WEST [ve] *$$*

Counter service
Organic vegan fast ;food.
V, MC
No alcohol

617 Ninth Avenue
bet. 43rd/ 44th Streets
646-998-3535
daily 8:30am-10pm

BLOSSOM DU JOUR--CHELSEA [ve] *$$*

Full Service
Vegan fast ;food.
Cash only
Organic beer, wine & sake
www. Blossomdujour.com

174 Ninth Avenue
bet. 20th/ 21st Streets
212-229-2595
daily 11:30am-10:30pm

"Shrewd Fast Food" is how Pamela Elizabeth describes her latest addition to her expanding vegan restaurant empire—Blossom Du Jour. It could equally be described as "Gourmet Fast Food." Fast it assuredly was: We had to wait only four minutes for a savory Gluten Free Quesadilla (spicy black beans, corn vegan cheese, and salsa) to appear; the Blossom Benedict Wrap followed in close order (Blossom's vegan version of Eggs Benedict slathered with a Hollandaise Sauce, and stuffed into a wrap.) Very tasty it was too. Over it, we uttered many benedictions.

Our next order arrived a minute later. This was the Midtown Melt (cajun-spiced seitan, vegan cheese, agave guacamole, lettuce, chipotle aoli). My companion had the aptly named Skyscraper (vegan burger, soy bacon, vegan cheese, onion rings, lettuce, tomatoes, pickles, special sauce), which also scaled the dizzying heights of gourmet fast foodism.

All four dishes were worthy of the gourmet vegan fare at Pamela's four other eateries: Blossom Dining. Blossom Café Uptown, Café Blossom and Blossom Bakery, not to mention her ex-husband Ronen's superb new vegan café, The V-Note, which has some dishes in common with the thtee Blossoms.

We consumed our meal while sipping chilled young coconut water, and gazing at the animal rights videos that were flickering on the video screen that is sunken into the wall above the small kitchen nook in the rear.

Blossom Du Jour occupies the former kitchen space of the adjacent Blossom Bakey. Since we are recovering vegan chocoholics, we were seduced by the aromas of vegan chocolate croissants that wafted through the partition that separates Blossom Du Jour Blossom Bakery. We fought the urge to conclude our very satisfying meal with some chocolate desserts at Blossom Bakery, but in the end gratefully succumbed.

BLOSSOM BAKERY [ve] $ 👍

Full Service
Vegan baked goods
All cards
No alcohol
www. Blossombakerynyc.com

174 Ninth Avenue
bet. 20th/ 21st Streets
212-242-3339
Tu-Th 9am-9pm
F-Sa 9am-10pm
Su 11am-8pm

"Blossom Village" is what Pamela Blackwell's friends teasingly call the complex of vegan eateries that she owns between 20th and 22nd Streets on 9th Avenue. Diagonally across the street from the wildly successful Blossom is Pamela's new vegan dessert emporium called Blossom Bakery. After dining spaciously next door at Blossom du Jour, we decided to cap off our meal with a Chocolate Croissant chased with a Cookie Dough mock milkshake. My companion, who is trying to be raw indulged her passion for sweets with a raw Key-Lime Pie over which she enthused.

CRISP-2 [v] $

Counter service
Israeli-Indian falafel shack
All major cards
No alcohol
Eatatcrisp.com

110 West 40th Street
bet. 6th Avenue / Broadway
212-661-0000
daily 10am-10pm
Sa-Su 12pm-8pm

CRISP-ON-WHEELS [v] $

Counter service
Israeli-Indian falafel truck
All major cards
No alcohol
www.Eatatcrisp.com

Corner 46th Street
bet. 5th/ 6th Avenues
212-661-0000
M-Th 11am-5pm
F 11am-3pm

See description under Midtown West; other location below Canal Street.

LOVING HUT [ve] $ 👍

Full service
Pan Asian
All Cards
No alcohol
www.lovinghutnyc.com

348 Seventh Avenue
bet. 29th/ 30th Streets
212-760-1900
M-Sa 9am-10pm
Breakfast 9am-11am

With its 160 branches world-wide, [with one opening every month, and more than 60 in the pipeline], Loving Hut is the fastest growing vegan restaurant chain in the world. Recently, one opened in Paris, and we ourselves have visited the ones in Houston, and San Francisco. The globe-girdling vegan restaurant chain, which started in Taiwan in 2008, is the brainchild of t Chinese-Vietnamese lady who has founded a spiritual movement whose mission it is to promote compassion for animals and to save the planet.

At least two months before opening the restaurant., each franchise owner has to become a practicing vegan. Each franchisee is also responsible for developing its own menu. Consequently, the food at each Loving Hut is markedly different. Despite the diversity of menus, the food at each Loving Hut franchise is of a uniformly high quality.

We tried their Vegan Joy (Five grain rice mixed with vegan chicken and mixed vegetables.) and found it very much to our liking. Then we downed their generous Crispy Vegan Burger. (Tomatoes, pickled cucumbers guacamole, romaine lettuce, oatmeal vegetable patty, burger sauce on a whole wheat bun).It comes with a side salad and is their best-selling menu item.. We finished our meal with a tapioca pudding topped with fresh mango chunks. Simply felicitous! Ally, the manager, told us that Loving Hut is trying to lure people away from their meat-centered diet with delicious vegan food. Based on the gustatory delights that we sampled at Loving Hut, we would say they're succeeding admirably.

MAOZ IV [v] $
Counter service
Israeli falafel shack, kosher
All Cards

200 W. 40th Street
at 7th Avenue
212-777-0820

MAOZ V [v] $
Counter service
Israeli falafel shack, kosher
All Cards
No alcohol
www.maozusa.com

683 8th Avenue
bet. 43rd/ 44th Streets
212-265-2315
daily 11am-12am

See description under Midtown East

MOSHE'S FALAFEL[ve] $

Food cart
Middle Eastern (Israeli), kosher
No cards
No alcohol

Corner 46th Street
at Sixth Avenue
(no phone)
M-Th 11am-5pm
F 11am-3pm

Let's face it: most falafel places in the city are just plain "foul-awful!" Mainly, we think, this is because of the cross-contamination. All-too-often, the "foul-awfuls" in non-veg. places are deep-fried in the same rancid oil that is used to cook animal flesh. At this outdoor food cart, however--because the food is vegan and kosher--none of these concerns apply.

Perhaps it was psychological, but knowing that the falafels weren't contaminated made them taste that much better. Evidently, Moshe's customers concur, because when we sampled his food, there was a line around the block! Portions are generous. Topped with colossal pickles, stuffed with chunks of tomato, fistfuls of lettuce, and drenched with the obligatory tahini sauce, Moshe's Falafels are fully twice the size of the standard-issue falafel sandwich. For those who like their falafels hot, ask for a devilishly piquant hot sauce on the side. Or if you're traveling any distance before eating it, ask for the tahini sauce on the side too. [The trick to eating a falalel sandwich is to eat it on the spot lest the tahini sauce seep into the bread and make it soggy. And nothing tastes worse than a soggy falafel sandwich!] Moshe serves up an ample salad and a selection of vegan soups as well.

NATURAL GOURMET COOKERY SCHOOL [ve] *$$$* 👍

48 West 21st Street
Full service   bet 5th and 6th Avenues
Gourmet vegan   212-645-5170
All cards   F 6:30pm
BYOB

Every Friday, the Natural Gourmet Cookery School has a feast that is prepared by the students at the school. The public is invited to partake of the students' cooking, which is vegan. Students, attired as waiters, serve four-course meals at large communal dining tables that are reminiscent of a college refectory. As in a college dining hall, the communal tables encourage the dinner guests to strike up conversations with total strangers, which adds to the convivial atmosphere.

The price for the four-course meal, may seem high, but then the cooking rivals that of any four-star restaurant. Truth to tell, we did overhear a few diners grumble about the meagerness of the portions. But the *nouvelle cuisine vegetarienne* style of cookery that is taught here dictates that portions be small. And the very fact that customers cry for more shows that the food is exceptionally tasty.

With the exception of only one item on the menu, we relished the food unreservedly. This was the Crispy Scallion Pancakes that were so crispy they tasted like hockey pucks. But the entree--Savory Baked Tofu Arame Stir-Fry with a Melange of Mushrooms and Fresh Vegetables in a Sweet and Spicy Sauce Served on a Bed of Lettuce and Crispy Rice Noodles--was divine. And the dessert! The dessert! Five Spiced Roasted Peach Pie with vegan Basil Ice-Cream and Sour Cherry Sauce, was sublime.

While everyone was clamoring for seconds and thirds on the vegan Basil Ice-Cream, the door to the kitchen suddenly swung open, and we saw something that we were not supposed to see. We spied the dessert chef downing a soup bowl filled with gobs of vegan Basil Ice-Cream. That's how good it was!

ONE LUCKY DUCK [v] *$$$* 👍

425 West 15th Street
Full Service   (Chelsea Market)
Gourmet organic raw food   212-255-4300
All major cards   M-Sa 10am-9pm
No alcohol   Su 10am-8pm

See review under Midtown East

ORGANIC AVENUE [ve] $$ 👍

Full service
Organic raw food boutiaue
All major cards
No alcohol
www.organicavenue.com

219 Eighth Avenue
at 21st Street
212-358-0500
M-F 7am-9pm
Sa-Su 9am-9pm

OTARIAN [v] $

Counter service
Global ovo-lacto vegetarian
All cards
No alcohol
www. Otarian.com

947 Eighth Avenue
at 56th Street
212-875-2600
M-Sa 11am-11pm
Su 11am-10pm

First of all, it's Otarian, not Oatarian.. The "O" is meant to symbolize the *orbis terrarum*. It might also symbolize the first letter of the surname of Radhka Oswal, the Perth-based vegetarian entrepreneur who has launched a chain of vegetarian fast food restaurants with the object of lowering the planet's carbon footprint. To this end, all the furnishings are made from recycled materials. The eating utensils are compostable. There is an LED monitor that demonstrates how one's food choices impact the planet. By eating Otarian's Tex-Mex Burger, for instance, we are told that it is the equivalent of driving an eco-friendly car.

Unfortunately, their Tex-Mex Burger like so many other items on the menu is not vegan. This is where their "eco-friendly" menu verges on hypocrisy. Otarian could dramatically reduce its carbon footprint by removing eggs and dairy products from its menu and going vegan. Dairy cows are a major source of green house gas emissions. They liberate methane, which is one of the deadliest of the greenhouse gases. Moreover, dairy products are cruelly exploitative of cows and are agriculturally unsustainable—to say nothing of their being detrimental to human health. [See Dr. T. Colin Campbell's *China Study (passim)* and Dr. Caldwell B. Esselestyn's *Prevent and Reverse Heart Disease (passim).*] One of the few items on the menu that was vegan was the Spicy Vegetable Noodles, We ate them with gusto. None of the desserts was vegan; so we had to forgo it.

Mr. Barlow, the manager, told us that he was wary of vegans because not a few vegans, when they learned that the menu contained eggs and dairy products, turned on their heel and stalked out. Perhaps it may seem that we are being hard on this ovo-lacto vegetarian restaurant. But when they congratulate themselves on their low carbon footprint, while continuing to serve eggs and dairy, they invite unsparing scrutiny.

•A recent visit, [in 2013], disclosed that although Otarian is still featuring food items that contain dairy, they've added more vegan options to the menu. We highly recommend their vegetable burgers, and their fries.

TERRI (Chelsea) [ve] **$** 👍

Counter service
Vegan Café (kosher)
All major cards
No alcohol
www.Terrinyc.com

60 West 23d Street
bet. Fifth/ Sixth Avenues
212-647-8810 ; 212-213-6068
M-F 6am-11pm
Sa,, Su 8am-4pm

Location is everything in the restaurant biz, and, in this respect, Terri is particularly well-favored. To the left, as you enter, it is flanked by an apartment building and to the right, it is flanked by a branch of HRC, In fact as we were downing our sandwiches, svelte ladies in leotards, who had just completed their gym workout strode in to slake their thirst with a juice cocktail; their hunger with a salad.

Founded by two former staff members off Blossom Uptown, Terri serves a delicious selection of vegan sandwiches, wraps, smoothies, as well as breads and baked goods that are baked on the premises. [Many of the baked goods are gluten free.] We shared a Roasted Vegetable Sandwich (eggplant, squash, sun-dried tomatoes, peppers, kalamata olives, and a dash of balsamic vinegar) served on Italian Rosemary Foccacio bread It was intensely flavorful. We followed   this   with   a   smoothie—The   Brazilian   Bombshell   (Acai, acerola,,blueberry,.mango,,banana, soymilk.) It doubled as a delicious dessert.

Although Terri rhymes with berry, we were puzzled as to why a vegan restaurant should bear the name Terri. It turns out that the two owners, Mike and Craig, dubbed the restaurant, Terri because, by coincidence, both their mothers are named Terri With the high quality of the vegan food dished up here, Craig and Mike have done their respective Terris proud.

See other location Below Canal Street

VEGGIETOPIA [v] **$**
Counter service
Israeli falafel shack
All Cards
No alcohol
www.veggietopia.com

578 Ninth Avenue
bet. 41st / 42nd Streets
212-967-1115
Daily 11am-10pm

Yet another Israeli falafel shack adorns the food landscape of New York City, but this one, we are chagrined to report is not up to the standard of Soom-Soom, or Moshe's (our favorites). The falafel sandwich itself was tasty enough, but the French fries served with it were so soggy and oily as to be inedible. Ditto for the samosa, which was overcooked   and greasy. On the plus side of the ledger, we liked the potato pancake and the Moroccan and Israeli salads; the sauces were merely okay. It's great that there is a vegetarian falafel shack in this rather gritty neighborhood, but the food is not superb. Veggie-Dystopia rather.

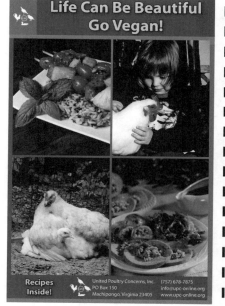
ZEN PALATE-HELL' S KITCHEN [v] **$$**

Full service
Asian vegetarian
All major cards
No alcohol
www.zenpalate.com

663 Ninth Avenue
at 46th Street
212-582-1669
daily 11:30am-10:45pm

This Zen Palate stands sentinel at the end of New York's restaurant row, providing the only palatable vegetarian option in the theater district. In the cozy, tastefully decorated interior, we love to dine on a pre-theater repast of Scallion Pancakes as an appetizer, followed by a main course of Mediterranean Medley (artichokes, basil, and tomatoes, stir-fried to perfection in a zesty garlic sauce). For dessert, it is our wont to have their scrumptious Chocolate-Raspberry Reincarnation. Now, properly fed, we're ready to watch the "strutters and fretters" on the boards of Broadway.

See other locations under Midtown East and Midtown West

MIDTOWN EAST and Gramercy Park
(East 14th to East 59th Streets)

BHOJAN VEGETARIAN [v] **$**

Full service
Kosher Vegetariah Gujerati / Punjabi
All cards
No alcohol
www. Bhojanny.com

102 Lexington Avenue
bet. East 27th/ 28th Streets
212-213-9615
daily 11:30am-10pm

Bhojan Vegetarian is noted for the generous portion size of its kosher vegetarian dishes that are prepared in the pungent style of Northeastern Indian cuisine—at reasonable prices. Their immense thalis are a meal unto themselves. We dined a la carte on some of their vegan entrees. We can highly recommend their Simla Aloo Gobi (spiced potatoes, cauliflower, and peppers); Tofu Jalfrezzi (spiced tofu, onions, bell peppers, mushrooms); and Maki Bindi (okra, onions, spices). It is good to see that they are using some tofu as a dairy substitute, but there is still a surfeit of dairy products on the menu.

BODY AND SOUL [v] **$**

Food stand
International, organic
No cards
No alcohol

Union Square Farmer's Market
at East 17th Street
212-982-5870
M, F 8am-6pm

One of the best ways to keep body and soul together in the city is to have a light vegan meal at the vegan food stand in the Union Square market, which is called aptly enough Body and Soul. Started by the owners of the late lamented Counter restaurant back in 1994, it draws throngs of hungry folk for breakfast, lunch, early light suppers, and snacks. And it's not hard to see why. The out-size wraps and turnovers are quite toothsome. Try the Saffron Potato wrap which teases the palate with plantain chunks hidden inside. Or try the Spinach Portabello Turnover, which is filled with tofu ricotta, and tastes a bit like a Spinach Lasagna. You might want to complement this with a dairy-free Blueberry Muffin, or a Sweet Potato Muffin. Don't leave the stand without biting into a melt-in-your-mouth Chocolate Brownie, or a Wheat-Free Almond Cookie. Then repair to one of the benches in Union Square Park and have an al fresco meal.

See other location in Brooklyn.

140 West 4th street
New York, NY 10012
1-212-260-1212

Red Bamboo
VEGETARIAN SOUL CAFE

CHENNAI GARDEN [v] **$$**
Full service
Kosher South Indian cuisine
All cards
No alcohol

129 East 27th Street
bet. Park/ Lexington Avenues
212-689-1999
Tu-F 11:30am-10pm
Sa, Su 12pm-10pm

Back in the late 1980s, Pradeep Shinde and Neil Constance, the two owners of this Curry Hill eatery, were among the first to open a kosher Indian vegetarian restaurant in New York. They were so successful that they retired to Orlando to take a flyer in the resort hotel business. They were successful there too, but they found that they pined for the fast tempo of New York City. So much so that they decided to collaborate on another kosher Indian vegetarian restaurant-- despite the heated competition.

 Their new joint venture is called Chennai Garden. The garden is a mere figure of speech (a row of plants that borders the front window), but Chennai is the pre-colonial name of Madras, the cultural capital of South India. And the restaurant breathes the pre-colonial spirit of South India before the Raj, when flesh food was an anomaly. Our palates were tickled by the Tamarind Pullao (rice perfumed with Tamarind and peanuts), the Bhindi Masala (okra curry) and the Behl Puri (a piquant mix of puffed rice, crisped noodles, onion and cilantro). In a nod to veganism, the Gulab Jamun, a flan which is usually made with powdered milk is made here with a powdered non-dairy mock milk. This makes Chennai garden the only Kosher Indian vegetarian restaurant where one may savor a vegan version of a traditional Indian dessert. The all-you-can-eat lunch buffet for $6.95 is one of New York's best restaurant bargains.

CRISP [v] **$**
Counter service
Israeli-Indian falafel shack
All major cards
No alcohol
Eatatcrisp.com

684 Third Avenue
at 43rd Street
212-661-0000
M-F 10am-9pm
Sa-Su 12pm-8pm

In this mid-Eastern vegetarian restaurant in mid-Eastern Manhattan, the word crisp is actually a euphemism for "falafel." Why substitute the word "crisp" for falafel? we asked the co-owner, Alan Kruvi, an Israeli, who was persuaded by his partner, Rakesh Barmecha, a Jain, to go veg. "Because falafels, as they are conventionally prepared, are greasy and low-end," says Alan. "Most falafel shops use the same oil. They never change it; they just add more oil to the original batch. We use fresh canola oil, and the oil is changed daily."

 And lo it was true: the falafel sandwiches in this sleek falafel,..er "crisp" shack are wonderfully crisp and fresh-tasting. The Basic Crisp arrives packaged in a biodegradable box that is cinched with a pull tab. Pull the tab and the box disgorges an hygienic, delectable falafel sandwich.

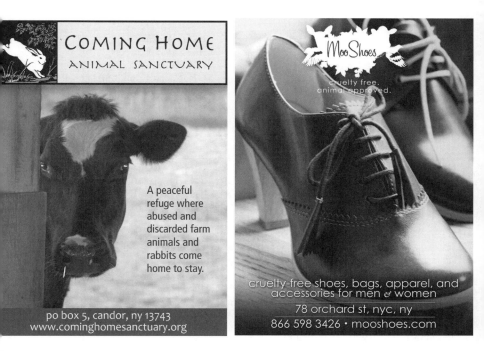
There are multiple falafel or "crisp" sandwiches on offer. Unfortunately, the only one that vegans can eat is the Basic Crisp. That's because all the others –the Mexican, the Mediterranean, the Parisian--are suffused in sauces that contain insidious ingredients like butter, milk, and cheese.

On the other hand, the Hummus Bowls, of which there are five, are all impeccably vegan. We had the Hummus Bowl with Sautéed Mushrooms [a concave dish of snowy hummus with a huge dollop of sautéed mushrooms in the center] and was quite fetched by it. Others to choose from include Hummus Bowls with Sautéed Eggplant, with Israeli Salad, and with Roasted Pepper.

Blended teas, sweetened with agave nectar, are paired with each dish. As in all the other falafel shacks in the city, there is the obligatory fresh lemonade served with a sprig of fresh mint.

All the utensils are compostable and bio-degradable. So just by virtue of eating here, one may make an ecological as well as an ethical affirmation, which is gratifying to the conscience as well as to the palate.

See other locations at Midtown West and Below Canal Street

FRANCHIA [ve] $$$

Full Service
Korean –inspired Asian fusion
All major cards
Oriental & Western Wines, Beers &
Soju cocktails
[Closing time designates last order]
www.Franchia..com/

12 Park Avenue
bet. 34th/ 35th Streets
212-213-1001
M-Th Lunch 12pm-3pm Dinner 4pm-10pm
F Lunch 12pm-3pm Dinner 4pm-10:15pm
Sa Lunch 1pm-3pm Dinner 4pm-10:15pm
Dinner only 5pm-9:30pm

Franchia is a vegan café, owned by William and Terri Choi, the people behind Hangawi, which Franchia rivals in elegance. Its name, Franchia, means "free, lavish, and generous." The interior space is nothing if not lavish. It is multi-tiered with a commanding ceiling. Decorated with colorful motifs, the ceiling is actually a replica of the ceiling from a Korean palace. Franchia is a refuge from the turmoil and hubbub of the city, where one may dine on delicious vegan fare in a Zen-like zone of tranquility.

Besides the wide selection of premium quality teas, Franchia also offers a delectable selection of vegan dishes comprising appetizers, salads, dumplings, noodles, wraps, bibimbap, stone bowl rice, main dishes and vegetarian sushis. Franchia's noodle dishes are especially interesting with selections such as sizzling spinach noodles, organic kale and brown rice noodles in a black bean sauce, Spicy Franchia Noodles, and many more.

By the way, Franchia is *the* place to come for bibimbap (the internationally renowned Korean rice dish that is topped with a variety of zesty vegetables.) At Franchia one may order bibimbap in a variety of selections, such as avocado, tofu, and vegetarian "duck." These may be served in a stone bowl, or in a bibimbap version.

Franchia also serves a wide selection of exotic teas, many of which are purported to have medicinal powers. Try 1st Picked Korean Wild Green Tea from the rocky slopes of Mt. Jilee, or 2nd Picked Mt. Guhwa Green Tea. For those who prefer herbal teas, there is a Ginger Tea, a Date Paste Tea, Korean Plum Tea and an Organic Dandelion tea.

High tea is observed at Franchia. Between lunch and dinner, one may also enjoy a relaxing afternoon tea at Franchia: The Royal tea tray entitles one to a starter choice of tea and an appetizer tray presenting vegetarian dumplings, pancakes, vegetarian sushi, zen rolls, vermicelli spring rolls, and stuffed mushrooms, a dessert tray.

With our Date Paste Tea, we ordered dinner that included an appetizer of their mouth-watering vegetarian dumplings. For a main course, we ordered the Tofu and Roasted Kabochah Pumpkin in sesame soy sauce with a side order of Avocado Bibimbap (Mixed rice wih avocado and vegetables served with bean paste sauce.) My partner had Soy 'Chicken' Sizzler on a Hot Plate with a side of Vegetarian 'Duck' in stone Bowl Rice, which she downed with gusto! For dessert, we had their incomparable Soy Cheese Cake with a dollop of Raspberry Sorbet. All of their dishes were exquisitely delicious and elegantly presented.

Franchia is also a popular place to hold bridal and baby showers. The bride-to-be is dressed in a traditional Korean bridal costume and shown how to brew tea in the traditional Korean way.

HANGAWI [ve] **$$$**

12 East 32nd Street

Full service
Korean
All major cards
Oriental and Western wines and beer &
Soju cocktails
[Closing time designates last order]
www.Hangawirestaurant.com

bet. Fifth/ Madison Avenues
212-213-0077 ; 212-213-6068
M-Th Lunch: 12pm-2:45pm Dinner:5pm-10:15pm,
F Lunch 12pm-2:45pm Dinner::5pm-10:30pm
Sa Lunch 1pm-3pm Dinner: 3pm-10:30pm
Su Dinner (only) 5 pm-9:30pm

Unless you've spent time in a Korean Buddhist monastery run by Alice Waters, you've never had food like this before. Slip off your shoes and experience a truly transporting zen dining experience [Make sure you are wearing attractive, clean socks!] Enter a zone of absolute harmony with the sounds of rushing wind and water filling the air, and prepare to be enchanted by an exotic menu of Korean vegan dishes: Grilled Todok (*Codonopsi Lanceolata*) [mountain root strips grilled in ginger soy sauce]; Organic Zen Bibimbap [assortment of organic mountain vegetables and greens over organic brown rice with hot chili paste.];Pumpkin Porridge; Ginseng Salad with bean paste dressing; Royal Green Tea.

Perhaps the best way to experience the unique flavors at Hangawi is to order the Emperor's Tasting Menu which brings you a variety of exquisitely presented vegan dishes. The service is impeccable and a meal at Hangawi always leaves you refreshed and buoyant.

The dishes presented in the Emperor's Tasting Menu changes monthly showcasing new creations by the chef.

There is also a seasonal menu highlighting some of the produce that is available during a particular season for eg the Matsutake Mushroom in the fall. Hangawi has been voted top vegetarian restaurant as well as top Korean restaurant for many years in Zagat's surveys

The owners of this superlative restaurant, William and Terri Choi, are devout Buddhists who come by their ethical vegan philosophy naturally. They are noted for their support of vegetarian and animal rights causes as much as for their devotion to the highest standards in food preparation and service.

KAJITSU $$$$

125 East 39th Street
bet. Park/ Lexington Avenues
212-228-4873
Dinner: T-Su 5:30pm-10pm
Lunch T-Sa 11:45-1;45pm

Full service
Japanese vegan haute cuisine
All major cards
Beer & sake
www.kajitsunyc.com

The food served at Kajitsu is pure *shojin ryori* or vegan food, which originated in the Buddhist temples of Japan. The dining area has the stark simplicity of a Kyoto temple, with geometric lines and light dappled wood surfaces. For lunch there are three choices, which range between $18 and $40. For dinner, there are two menus: One is a four-course $55 one. The other is an eight-course $85 one. Except for the Housemade Soba Noodles, which are a constant, the menus change monthly and feature food items that look penitential and austere, but in the hands of chef Masato Nishihara, are transformed into dishes that are interesting and flavorful, albeit a touch too salty for our taste.

We opted for the more expensive menu and were regaled with such dishes as Agar Agar Aspic with Summer Vegetables Served with Umami Soy Sauce. (Liliputian summer vegetables were suspended in a tasty soy-sauce-soaked gelatinous goo.) This was followed by a hearty Celery Root Soup that was flavored with red daikon and kohlrabi. We especially liked the next courses--poached tomatoes, the tempura vegetables and the corn croquettes. The dominant flavor note in all the dishes is saltiness, Even the dessert--Sweetened Edamame Mochi with Pistachio Nuts--smacked of salt.

The owners of Kajitsu, self-admittedly, are aiming to attract food snobs and gastronomes. This is reflected in the price of the food, which is as redolent of the temples of commerce as the Zen temples of Kyoto. Our bill at the end of the meal, including tax and tip, was hefty . Eating at Kajitsu then, in addition to being a transcendent dining experience is an exercise in conspicuous consumption. Perhaps this is not a bad thing. Veganism will advance socially only when it is invested with snob appeal. After all high status feeders, never question the price of an entrée at pretentious carnivorous restaurants, So one should consider the food here, which is so painstakingly prepared, to be cheap at the price.

MADRAS MAHAL [v] $$

Full service
Indian vegetarian, kosher
Major cards
Beer & wine

104 Lexington Avenue
bet. 27th/28th Streets
212-684-4010
Su 12pm-10pm, F 11:30am-3pm
M-Th 11:30am3pm & 5:30pm-10pm

The menu asks for your patience since the food is freshly prepared. Maybe that includes scything the wheat for chapatis. At any rate, it took 45 minutes to get drinks and an hour for samosas which were hot and flaky, with the rich taste of freshly ground spices. After another half hour we got Kala Chana (black chick pea curry) and Sukhi Bhaji (potato stir fried with hot pepper, dry fruit and nuts). But we were cranky after waiting so long, and the dishes didn't measure up to our expectations, especially at nine dollars apiece.

MAOZ [v] $

Counter service
Israeli falafel shack, kosher
All Cards
No alcohol
www.maozusa.com

638 Union Square East
bet. 16th/ 17th Streets
212-260-1988
daily 11am-12am

Like a green shoot in a bowl of sprouting chick-peas, Maoz joins the other vegetarian falafel shacks in Manhattan--Crisp, Taim, Hummus Place, Moishes, et al, that have sprung up, seemingly overnight.

Oblong and solidly built, Maoz looks like nothing so much as a bunker, which is exactly what Maoz means in Hebrew. The "bunker" looks eminently capable of fending off carnivorous its food. Another potent weapon is the undeniable fact that vegetarian fast food is healthful: It's the only fast food that isn't fat food. Rather, it's fit food. Eat as many salads and as many falafel sandwiches as you like and you'll still be slender.

All the food is prepared on the premises. The most popular item on the menu, which accounts for 80 percent of the sales is the Maoz salad, which one may assemble from as many as twenty healthful ingredients. Such as pickled eggplant, pickled carrot salad, couscous with parsley, shredded cabbage, onion and tomato salad, olives and, assorted pickles, special broccoli and cauliflower salads.

Add five falafel balls to the above ingredients, and you can construct a falafel salad. Add five falafel balls, and make yourself a Maoz falafel sandwich. We savored the Maoz Royal, which contained assorted salad ingredients plus eggplant and humus.

Bunkers and vegetarianism would seem to be incompatible notions, but, according to Nat Hirshman and his daughter. there are already 32 vegetarian bunkers in Europe. When you stop to consider it: a bunker is a zone of tranquility, an oasis of peace in a hostile world. And that's what Maoz is--a gustatory peace bunker that promises to spread and swallow New York.

See other locations under East Village and Upper West Side.

ONE LUCKY DUCK [v] $$$

Full Service
Gourmet organic raw food
All cards
No alcohol
www.oneluckyduck.com

125 1/2 East 17th Street
bet. 3rd Avenue/ Irving Place
212-477-7151
daily 11am-11pm

This is the vest-picket version of Pure Food and Wine with many of the menu items at PFW available for take-out. Here, you can get one of Pure Food's tastiest dishes, the Zucchini and Tomato Lasagna with Basil Pesto and Pignoli Ricotta. Their Flatbread Pizza with Hummus, Avocado and Mint Pesto makes a delectable take away lunch, as does our favorite Tortilla Wrap with Chili Spiced 'Beans' The juice bar offers some exotic juice combinations such as Hot Pink (Beet Pineapple, Watermelon and Ginger) and smoothies. Try the Green Mango Shake (Mango, Fresh Coconut Water and a dash of Vanilla). Many of the desserts served at Pure Food are also offered here. We were glad to see the Toco Coco Brownies. And we also liked the Fruit, Granola and Vanilla Cream Parfait. The desserts, as at Pure Food, are made without honey. Making a commendable effort to be consistently vegan, they use Agave Nectar and Maple Syrup instead of honey. However, their use of bee pollen as a supplement keeps them from being impeccably vegan

See other location under Midtown West.

ORGANIC AVENUE [ve] $$

Full service
Organic raw food boutiaue
All major cards
No alcohol
www.organicavenue.com

649 Lexington Avenue
bet. 54th/ 55th Srreets
212-358-0500
M-Sa 7am-8pm
Sa Su 9am-6pm

PONGAL[v] $$

Full service
Indian vegetarian
Major cards
No alcohol

110 Lexington Avenue
bet. 27th and 28th St.
212-696-9458
M-Th 11:30am-10:30pm
F-Su 11:30am-11pm

Yes, the Big Apple boasts some of the finest Indian vegetarian cuisine this side of the Indus River. Night after night, one can eat in one great Indian restaurant after another without feeling that one has dined redundantly. The dining experience at Pongal is incomparable. Start with appetizers called Kachoori, then progress to a roll-your-own-crepe called Paper Dosa. This is a

THANKSVEGAN

A VEGAN COOKBOOK FOR
THE HARVEST HOLIDAY

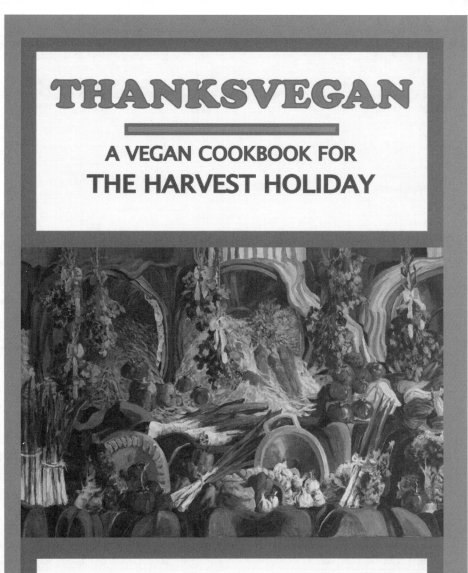

Roberta Kalechofsky & Roberta Schiff

large Indian crepe made of rice flour and served with spiced potato on the side. The trick to rolling your own crepe is to tear off bits of dosa; fill them with the spicy potato mixture then dip them into a fresh coconut chutney. All dishes are served on banana leaves. Undhiya a Gujarati dish that we sampled is highly recommended containing as it does such exotic ingredients as yam, lotus root, potatoes and eggplant. When we'd polished off this and the okra-tomato curry, the waiter brought us Kachooris (deep-fried puffs of Toor dal lentil and Bathata Dada). We finished the meal with a decaf coffee from Madras. We forbore to have any of the tempting desserts as none (alas! alack!) was vegan. So we sauntered down to Lula's for a vegan ice-cream.

See other location under Upper East Side.

PURE FOOD AND WINE (v) $$$ 👍

Full service
Gourmet organic raw food
All cards
Organic beer & wines

54 Irving Place
bet. 17th/ 18th Streets
212-477-1010
M-Su 12pm-3pm
M-Su 5:30pm-11pm

With the opening of Pure Food and Wine the preparation of raw food has reached its apogee in New York, if not the world. The food, which is nearly, but not quite totally vegan and raw, (except for the bee pollen, which is offered as a supplement), shows off the virtuosity of two talented New York chefs--Sarma Melngailis and Matthew Kenney (formerly of Matthews on the Upper East Side). In previous incarnations, both had won fame as chefs de cuisine cooking animal flesh for carnivores. But suddenly, about six years ago, over dinner at the rawfoods restaurant Quintessence, they had a simultaneous epiphany; they realized that eating vegan rawfood was better for their health, better for the health of animals, and better for the ecological health of the planet. Hence their motto, which they proudly display on the front page of their menu: "Handcrafted flavors that rejuvenate the body, mind, and planet."

A hard-bitten skeptic might scoff that chefs who excelled at making dead animal parts taste yummy should have no trouble infusing raw vegetable and fruit concoctions with flavor. Just so. This is why the food at Pure Food and Wine surpasses that of any other rawfood restaurant that we have visited. These two chefs have applied the *hautest* techniques of nouvelle cuisine to the preparation of rawfoods, and the results are truly sensational.

We can unreservedly recommend all the dishes that we tasted. Start with the Thai Lettuce Wraps that come with a spicy tamarind dipping sauce. Another appetizer to try is the Tomato Tartare with Kaffir Lime. For a main course, try the Beet Ravioli--[Rectangles of thinly sliced beets sandwiched together with a cashew nut filling]. Or the Golden Squash Pasta with Summer Black Truffles [Spiralized Yellow Squash slathered with a hearty truffle sauce with sweet peas and chervil]. For dessert, we commend to your tastebuds Chewy Dark Chocolate Cookie with Chocolate and Pistachio Ice Creams [This is a soft cookie, served with candied pistachios, strawberry sauce, and dollops of vegan ice-cream made from nut cream.]

The restaurant's interior is plush, and the walls are decorated with pictures of happy

The eating of animal flesh extinguishes the great seed of compassion

THE BUDDHA (SIDDHARTHA GAUTAMA OR SHAKYAMUNI)
563 BC–483 BC from *The Mahaparinirvana*

all creatures great and small

Millions of Americans love animals. But many creatures still suffer from cruel and abusive treatment.

Help us confront animal cruelty in all its forms. Visit **humanesociety.org** to find out what you can do.

Celebrating Animals | Confronting Cruelty

THE HUMANE SOCIETY
OF THE UNITED STATES

animals (pleased, no doubt, because they're not being eaten). The spacious patio is the perfect setting for the eating of things raw. Here one may dine al fresco, and in the event of a sudden downpour waiters are adept at setting up huge parasols that protect the diners from precipitation. The atmosphere is so convivial that strangers talk to each other across tables. Sitting next to us were two non-vegetarian women who were prolonging their meal by ordering endless glasses of coconut water and organic wine--because they couldn't tear themselves away from the place. It's that magnetic!

Not content to rest on their laurels, Kenney and Melngailis have collaborated on an uncook book, *Raw Food/ Real World: 100 Recipes to Get the Glow*, which tells one how to reconstruct the dishes that are on offer in the restaurant. Published by Regan Books, it became an instant bestseller. Early in 2006, Sharma and Matthew parted ways. Sharma continues to run Pure Food with her customary élan and Matthew has gone on to start a raw culinary school – cum-café in Oklahoma City called 100 Degrees Haute. He's also penned two more raw books: *Everyday Raw*, and *Entertaining in the Raw*.

SARAVANA BHAVANA (v) $ 👍

Full service	81 Lexington Avenue
Chennai home style	at 26th Streets
All major cards	212-679-0204
Wine & beer	Lunch Tu-Su 12m-4pm
	Dinner 5:30pm-10pm

Saravana Bhavan--Englished means "house of Saravana". Brother of Ganesh, the elephant god of prosperity, Sarvana seems to be shedding a benign protection on this house. And according to the manager, Ms. Ramaya, they will need every ounce of Saravanaas' help. There is fierce competition with other Indian restaurants on Curry Hill, and there appears to be a jinx on the street corner where Saravanaas is located.. So far, every restaurant that has occupied this corner has failed.

But if the quality of the food and the service are anything to go by, Saravanaas will beat the odds. Already, the place is packed with frugal diners, both Indian and Western, who obviously recognize a bargain when they eat one. Modestly priced, and
highly flavorsome, the cuisine--Chennai homestyle--is the type of food that one might encounter at a home in Chennai (formerly Madras). The menu abounds in delicious dosas, uthapams, vadas, and thalis redolent of India's deep south. Nearly all the dishes are cooked in oil, not ghee (clarified butter). But vegans must beware of the Iddly (Steamed Rice and Lentil Patty), which is topped off with a ladleful of ghee. Also, the Sambars in the Thalis are sometimes flavored with ghee.

For an appetizer, we had the Sambar Vada (Crispy Lentil Doughnuts in a Mild, Spicy South Indian Soup, Garnished with Onion and Cilantro). For the main course, we had the Dried Fruit Rava Dosa (a mildly spiced Crepe made of Wheat and Rice Flour, blended with Whole Raisins, Pistachios, and Cashews). This we dipped into three different coconut-based chutneys and a sambar. Verboten to vegans are the desserts. As in most Indian restaurants, they are highly caseous, containing ghee, milk, yogurt, and cheese.

Unlike other restaurants on Curry Hill, Saravanaas refuses to use frozen vegetables and will not serve leftovers. Ms. Ramaya told us that all the vegetables are purchased from local Indian suppliers. This accounts for the high quality and astonishing freshness of each dish. Saravana Bhavan is actually the New York branch franchise of a chain of successful Indian vegetarian restaurants that originate in Chennai. So all the dishes are made to standards set by the home office in Chennai. This can have its drawbacks. When we asked for soy milk to be used in a Lassi, or in an Indian coffee, which is pre-mixed with cow's milk, the manager told us that the home office does not permit its franchises to substitute soy milk for cow's milk. This strikes us as a silly practice-- especially as the home office has allowed the New York franchise to serve wine and beer, which no other restaurant in the chain is allowed to do. So, it is incumbent that vegans politely demand soy milk for their lassis and coffees.[If the Starbucks chain,--which is non-veg.-- can offer soymilk, then why not Saravana Bhavana, which is veg.?] Apart from this notable lapse, the service is faultless, and the food is very good value for the money.

SOFT SERVE FRUIT CO, THE [v] $

Counter service
Soft serve shack
All cards
No alcohol
www.softservefruitco.com

25 East 17th Street
 bet. W. Union Square/ Broadway
212-675-0550
M-Th,Su 7:30am-10:00pm
F,Sa 7:30am-12am

See description under Upper East Side.

SQUEEZE, THE(ve) $

Counter service
Raw vegan food truck
All cards
www. Thesqueeze..com

Parked on East 17th Street
 bet. Broadway/ 5th Avenue
646-598-8502
Daily 7:30am-9pm

Such is the population density and cultural diversity of NYC that it has become a city of culinary firsts. For instance, it's the first city that we know of that boasts an Indian restaurant that is vegan. Actually, it's a restaurant on wheels, a food cart called New York Dosas. NYC is also the first city to boast a vegan doughnut shop--Dun-Well Doughnuts in Williamsburg, Brooklyn. Now, New York City boasts the first raw vegan food truck—The Squeeze.

Located in Union Square West, usually the penultimate in a convoy of food trucks idling curbside--The Squeeze was founded by Karla Brooks, an NYU alumna with degrees in nutrition and broadcast journalism. The raw food that she has crafted is very tasty, and rivals that of Pure Food & Wine. We started with the Meatballs, which is rather unappetizingly and ineptly named, but was very tasty. Its meaty flavor derives from the raw crimini mushrooms that it contains; and its cheesy sauce is based on soaked cashews. A variant of this dish is the Open Faced Meatloaf Sandwich (also crimini-mushroom based), served on gluten free bruschetta. Next we tried the raw vegan hot dogs; however, in mid-prep, Max, the counterman told us that the vegan hot dogs were not really raw; albeit the fixings are raw, the weiner itself--made from vegetable protein-- is cooked. Ditto for the Mac and Cheese: the noodles are made from Quinoa, but are decidedly cooked; but the cashew cheese sauce, in which they are a-swim, is raw. [Max, the counterman, told us that these were the only two cooked items on the menu.]

Since the food truck's name is The Squeeze, we were eager to sample the squeezed stuff—the smoothies, the pressed juices, and the boosters. There wasn't one that we didn't toss off with gusto! Our favorite booster was the Anti-Aging booster (raw, un-pasteurized coconut water, acai berries, goji berries, aloe vera). Our favorite pressed juice was My Plastic Surgeon Got Laid Off...By ME (cucumber juice, aloe vera, and E3 Live). Our favorite smoothie was the Blueberry Hemp Milk (alkaline water, blueberry, hempseed, cashew, vanilla bean, dates.) Delicious, healthful raw, vegan comfort food, not to say junk food, is what Karla is striving for. And we would say that she has succeeded admirably. Such has been the success of The Squeeze that Karla has laid plans to organize a fleet of raw vegan Squeeze trucks and dispatch them all over the city. Look for the next one to open on Wall Street and for a storefront to squeeze into a space in Williamsburg hard by Dun-Well doughnuts.

TIFFIN WALLAH [v] $

Counter service	127 East 28th Street
Mumbai homestyle	bet. Park/ Lexington Avnues
All Cards	212-685-7301
Beer & wine	M-Su 11:30am-3:00am
www.tiffinwallah.us	M-Su 5pm-10pm

What is a tiffin wallah.? We asked Pradeep Shinde, owner of this eating establishment of the same name. An institution peculiar to Mumbai--which is where Pradeep grew up.--"tiffin wallah," is a man who fetches vegetarian lunches made by Mumbai housewives; he then ferries them to their husbands in their city offices. Pradeep wanted to import this concept to New York in a slightly modified form. So he sees the restaurant as a sort of communal "tiffin wallah," conveying homestyle vegetarian meals to New York City's office workers.

Trained as an engineer in Mumbai, Pradeep moved to New York where he switched his major to hotel management at NYU. For a time, after his graduation, he worked as a personal butler at the Park Lane Hotel. Then, he started his own restaurant, Madras Mahal, which was the first vegetarian restaurant on Curry Hill. (Now there are seven.)

Tiffin Wallah hums with efficiency. Pradeep is everywhere at once, recalling his buttlilng days; he bustles about, overseeing the minutest detail. He wipes a spot of gravy from a bin cover, then he replenishes the salad bowls. A small but diligent wait staff is poised to do his bidding.

At lunch, the place is thronged with young, and middle-aged professionals who rhapsodize over the six-dollar buffet--the best luncheon deal in town. When we asked him how long he would peg the price at six dollars, Pradheep promised us, perhaps with a touch of hyperbole, that this price would be fixed in perpetuity.

On weekends, Tiffin Wallah serves exotic dosas (crepes) that cannot be found anywhere else. We recommend the Pesaratu, a dosa made from green lentils and green chilies; the Spring Dosa, which is a mixed vegetable dosa; and the Jaipur Masala Dosa.

At the buffet, we could eat only the Chana Masala, and a vegetable sabji. The other dishes, save for the delicious, small stuffed vegetable Uttapam, were caseous. Since many of our readers are persnickety vegans, as we are, they are reluctant even to eat in places where mammary secretions are served. So we extracted from Pradeep a promise that he would be willing to make mock meat substitutions for any caseous a la carte item. We urged him to visit Desi Junction, which, albeit a working-man's Indian restaurant, they nonetheless have integrated soy into a number of their formerly caseous dishes.

VATAN [v] $$$ 🖐

	409 Third Avenue
Full service	at 29th Street
Indian	212-689-5666 (reservations essential)
(V, MC)	Tu-Su 5:30pm-10pm
Full bar	Closed Mondays

At first glance, $31.00 *prix fixe* may seem like a lot of rupees, but think of a visit to Vatan as a cut-price ticket to India. The decor instantly transports you to a village in Gujarat, where costumed waiters and waitresses look as if they've just popped out of Aladdin's lamp to do your bidding. At the snap of your fingers, they will bring you all the appetizers you can eat; and the appetizers are so indescribably scrumptious, you'll eat yourself into a stupor. We stuffed ourselves unashamedly with delicate miniature samosas filled with peas and potatoes, the Chana Masala (chick peas with onions and coriander) and an array of Indian breads such as papadams and puris, but still found room for a rich dessert of Mango Rus (mango pulp). The music, authentic Indian ragas, is soft and unobtrusive. The food is prepared with canola oil, not ghee. The service is faultless.

ZEN PALATE [v] $$ 🖐

	516 Third Avenue
Full service	bet. 34th/ 35th Streets
Asian vegetarian	212-685-6888
All major cards	

ZEN PALATE [v] $$ 🖐

	115 East 18th Street
Full service	brt/ Park Avenue/ Irving Place
Asian vegetarian	212-387-8885
All major cards	daily 11:30am-10:45pm
No alcohol	
www.zenpalate.com	

See description under Midtown West and other location under Midtown West.

🖐 Indicates we especially recommend this restaurant for the quality of the food.

GREENWICH VILLAGE

(Houston Street to West 14th Street, Hudson River to Fifth Avenue)

CAFÉ BLOSSOM [ve] *$$$* 👍

Full Service
Global vegan, orgainc
All cards
Organic spirits; full bar
www.blossomnyc.com

41 Carmine Street
bet. Bleecker/ Bedford Streets
646-438-9939
daily 11:30am-10:30pm

The first thing you see when you enter Café Blossom on Carmine Street, is a quote from the noted AR attorney Gary Francione: "Vegan is not a diet, it's a pleasure." We can attest that nothing could be more voluptuous than a vegan meal at Café Blossom on Carmine Street. We started with exquisite Cashew cheese dumplings, which were steamed and served with a tamari plum sauce. As a main course, we ordered Southern Fried Seitan with steamed kale and a daiya cheese biscuit that had the consistency of mashed potatoes. It was a fascinating concatenation of flavors that reached a crescendo with the Passionfruit Cheesecake that we had for dessert.

GOBO [ve] *$$* 👍

Full service
Asian-Western fusion cuisine
All cards
Organic beer & wine
www.goborestaurant.com

402 Sixth Avenue
at 8th Street
212-255-3242
Su-We 11:30am-11:30pm
Th-Sa 11:30am-12am

Gobo is proof of the fact that one can be a principled vegetarian yet enjoy the most exquisite food. For the food at Gobo's outstrips the cuisine of its parent restaurant Zen Palate. (This is ironic because most of the dishes were created by Mrs. Wu, the co-owner of Zen Palate). We started our dinner with a smoothie called The Awakening (mango, cherry and wolfberry), which was truly ambrosial. With our taste buds duly awakened, we were in a fit condition to enjoy the entrees, which were also very much to our taste--Sizzling Soy Cutlet Platter with Black Pepper Sauce, and the Soy Filet with Coconut Curry Rice. The desserts, all of which are vegan, were also extraordinary. We relished the Multi-layered Chocolate Cake and the Coconut-Chocolate Pudding with Mango Puree.

There are two non-vegan dishes--Avocado Tartare, which contains honey; and Crispy Spinach and Soy Cheese Wontons, which contains casein, a cows' milk extract, and egg, an ingredient in the won ton wrappers. Cow's milk, alas, is also available to tea and coffee drinkers who prefer it to the soy milk that is on offer.

The talk is that, if it is successful, Gobo plans to franchise the restaurant. Judging from the impeccable service, the attractive decor and the exquisite food, the burdock will soon be taking root in other American cities.

See other location under Upper East Side.

HUMMUS PLACE I [v]$

Full Service
Israeli vegetarian, kosher

99 Macdougal Street
bet. W. 3rd/ Bleecker Streets
212-533-3089

HUMMUS PLACE IV [v] $

Full Service
Israeli vegetarian, kosher
All cards
Wine & Beer

71 7th Avenue South
bet. Barrow/Bleecker Streets
212-924-2033
Su-Th 11am-12am
Fr-Sa 11am-2am

New York already has single-food-item restaurants dedicated to the French Fry, the Falafel, the Baked Potato, the Crepe, the Dosa, the Pancake, the Doughnut, Popcorn, Soup, and the Noodle; there is even a Candy bar (Dylan's)--so why not a restaurant devoted soley to Hummus? At Hummus Place, a tidy little beanery with walls the color of tahini, you can order two different styles of hummus--one made from fava beans and chickpeas, Hummus Foul (pronounced fool), and the other made from whole chickpeas, Hummus Masabacha. The fava beans and the chickpeas are imported from Israel to insure quality and freshness. The beans are then set to soak overnight and are chopped up in a huge Robotcoupe; then cooked for a full five hours. The hummus is served with a snow white tahini which is also imported from Israel.Two of the dishes are made with eggs; so vegans must tell the chef to hold the eggs!

Fittingly enough, the man who founded Hummus Place is an Israeli named Ori Apple, formerly of Kibbutz Maoz Haim. After his army service in Israel, Apple alighted in the Big Apple to study cooking at the French Culinary Institute in Soho. Having worked for a number of restaurants and a catering service in the city, Apple decided to strike out on his own. With the help and advice of his best friend--(now co-owner and chef of Hummus Place)--Nitzan Raz, Apple started Hummus Place. Apple's hummus is considered to be so authentic that Israelis joke that they no longer have any reason to visit Tel Aviv.

Because they've been cooked to a fare-thee-well-well, the flavor of the hummuses are a bit bland. Luckily, they come with a hot sauce on the side with a secret recipe whose base is cilantro. We found that the judicious seasoning of hummus with hot sauce enlivens the flavor

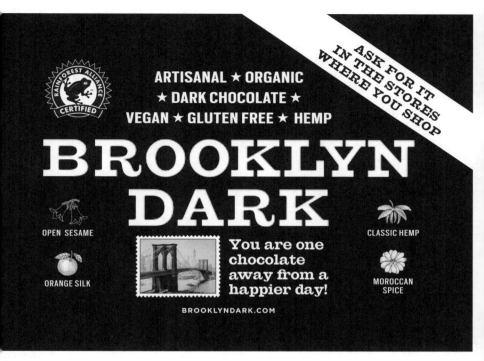
and makes it go down much better. The hummus also comes with an Israeli Salad (whose ingredients are not imported from Israel). To give it an added fillip, we tried mixing the Israeli Salad in with the hummus and the hot sauce Then we used; the resultant mixture to fill a whole wheat pita pocket, which came with our order. This worked splendidly. We washed it all down with a cool glass of refreshing lemonade (also made with a secret recipe) that contains a sprig of fresh Israeli Mint. At the end of our meal, we left feeling satisfied and full of beans.

See other locations under East Village, MidTown West, and Upper West Side.

INTEGRAL YOGA NATURAL FOODS [ve] $

Take-out counter
International
All cards
No alcohol
www. iynaturalfoods.com

229 West 13th Street
bet. 7th/ 8th Avenues
212-243-2642
M-F 8am-9:30pm
Sa 8am-8:30pm
Su 9am-8:30pm

Integral Yoga was started by Swami Satchidananda back in the seventies. The Swami taught that it was bad karma to consume or purvey animal flesh. Consequently, Integral Yoga is one of the few health food stores in the city that doesn't peddle flesh. Now you can tap into their good karma by having a meal there. Nestled into the North West corner of the store is one of the city's best vegan buffets. You may choose from such selections as Curried Black-Eyed Peas, Hot and Spicy Tofu and Bok Choy with Almonds. There is also a juice bar where you may purchase soups and veggie burgers. If you're a rawfoodist, take heart! There's a capacious salad bar; and in a refrigerated display case next to the buffet, there is an appetizing selection of raw vegetable pies, fruit pies, cakes, and cookies.

NEW YORK DOSAS[ve]$

Washington Square Park
Food cart   West 4th/ Sullivan Streets
South Indian   917-710-2092
No cards   M-Sa 11am-4pm
No alcohol

We had to stand in line behind ten people to give our order to Thiru Kumar, the chef who works his magic at this outdoor food cart. Our order was for a Masala Dosa (a rolled rice-flour crepe stuffed with spicy potato mixture), Jafna Dosa (a rolled rice-flour crepe stuffed with Sambahl); Ponidicherry Utapam (a flat bread topped with fresh, chopped vegetables); and Iddly with Sambar (an Indian biscuit made from lentil flour and dipped in a spicy Sambar or soup).

Thiru, a native of Sri Lanka, works fast; he pours a batter made from crushed fermented rice and lentils on the griddle and within a few seconds, Utapam and Dosas appear, as if by magic. He fills them with spicy mashed potatoes and chopped fresh vegetables--and the result dosas and utapams worthy of the finest Indian restaurants.

Thiru packed our order into boxes; then we sat on a bench in Washington Square park and savored every morsel.

It's hard to believe that so much food can pour forth from one little food cart! In addition to the Dosas, one may order Samosas with vegetable fillings; Medhu Vada (lentil donuts), and the aforementioned Iddly with Sambar. Thiru also offers up a unique array of tinned fruit juices imported from Thailand--such as Rambutan juice, Longan juice, and, our favorite, Lychee juice-- that are available nowhere else in the city. Unusual for an Indian food establishment, vegans may dine here without having to ask about objectionable ingredients--as all the food is 100 per cent vegan. [Thiru bowed to pressure from vegan students at the NYU Vegan Society to make his food cart exclusively vegan. Now he himself has turned vegan.]

ORGANIC AVENUE [ve] $$

Self service   43 8th Avenue
Organic raw food bar/boutique   bet. Jane/ /Horatio Streets
All major cards   212-358-0500

No alcohol

www.organicavenue.com

daily 8am-8pm

See description under SOHO.

RED BAMBOO [ve] $$ 👍

Full service
Asian soul food fusion
All cards
No alcohol
www.redbamboo-nyc.com

140 West 4th Street
bet. 6th/MacDougal
212-260-1212
M-F 12:30pm-12am
Sa-Su 12pm-12am

"Soul Food with Asian overtones" is how the proprietor, Philip Wong, describes the cuisine A
play here are multi-ethnic flavors such as Chinese, Korean, Thai, Indian. Creole and Soul Food
In most instances, the fusion of flavors works.

For appetizers, we had the Caribean Jerk Spiced Seitan, which was tangy and tasty, a
were the Collard Green Rolls, the Popcorn Shrimp, and the gluten "pork" in the Tonkatsu Chops
We also sampled the Mango Chicken. and the Barbecue Buffalo Wings, which were finge
lickin' good. However, on the debit side, the Seoul Pancake was too mushy and the sweet corr
mashed potatoes were way too bland. We capped it all off with a scrumptious Death By
Chocolate cake served with a dollop of vegan Mint Chocolate Chip ice-cream. The waiters were
attentive and hovering.

The only difficulty that vegans might have with eating at Red Bamboo is that the menu is
so unrelievedly mock-carnivorous that the mere sight of dishes with names like Satay Chicken
Popcorn Shrimp, and Roast Beef Sandwich, no matter how mock, might conjure unpleasan
associations with the real thing. Nonetheless, Red Bamboo is a great place to take your meat
eating friends to show them how animal flesh may be mocked to perfection. Two dishes contain
dairy and these are noted on the menu.

ROCKIN' RAW [v] $$ 👍

Full service
Peruvian-New Orleanian organic raw food
All major cards
Full bar
www.rockinraw.com

171 Sullivan Street
bet. Houston / Bleecker Streets
917-337-5776
T-Sa 2pm-9pm
Su 1pm-9pm

Luis Salgado of Lima, Peru and Tere Fox of New Orleans, Louisiana met at a rock concert, and
shortly thereafter, they enrolled as students at the Institute of Integrative Nutrtition, of which
they are alumni. Soon after graduating, they decided to merge their talents and their knowledg
of their native cuisines to open a Peruvian-Creole raw food restaurant where they created some
of the most innovative vegan raw food dishes in the city,

However, after four years of doing a thriving business in Williamsburg, they decided to move their operation to Manhattan. For three principle reasons: a) their client base is in Manhattan; b) the L-train, which connects Manhattan to Williamsburg, was subject to frequent service interruptions; c) they wanted to be closer to the epicenter of raw food cuisine, which is in lower Mahnattan. On their new menu, they've included modified versions of some of their greatest hits from the RR in Williamsburg, including the ever-popular Raw Po Boy, etc.

The ambience at RR's new location is reminiscent of the former one *sans* the bosky garden; but the food, if possible, is even better. We commenced with their starter Fully Loaded Nachos: Seasoned flax-seed chips are freighted with seed cheeses, mock raw sour cream, lettuce tomato, and avocado bits. The portion is so generous, and satisfying as to be a meal unto itself. We followed this with a spicy raw spaghetti (actually spiralized zucchini) that Luis has dubbed *Talairenas ala Huancaina* . The zucchini noodles are a-swim in a sauce made from Peruvian yellow pepper and nuts. A mound of dressed zucchini strands is served sprinkled with mushrooms and *cholos* (large, button-size kernels of Peruvian corn).

Between bites, we slaked our thirst with a Cucumber Mojito, and a Watermelon Cooler. Both were deeply refreshing--followed by a Chocolate and a Strawberry Smoothie (made with home-made almond milk) which were most exhilarating.

We capped off the meal with their raw strawberry short cake, for which the adjective, scrumptious, was devised. Luis told us that RR supplies Organic Avenue and other emporia with a range of their raw sweets and savories, which are so popular that these places find it difficult to keep them in stock. It's not hard to see why.

SACRED CHOW [v]$$ 👍

Full service
International, organic, & bakery
V, AE, MC
Organic beer & wine
www.sacredchow.com

227 Sullivan Street
bet. West 3rd & Bleecker Streets
212-337-0863
M-F 9 am--11pm
Sa-Su 11:30am-11pm

Cliff Preefer, the owner of Sacred Chow used to be the head chef as well as the pastry chef, at Candle Cafe back in the mid-90's. Then he decided to strike out on his own and start a veg. delicatessen, which eventually gave place to this new restaurant of the same name. Casting about for a name for his eatery, he hit upon the inspired pun--"sacred chow." With its logo of the meditating cow, and its pun on sacred cow, could Cliff's restaurant have been anything but vegan? Unfortunately, yes. Cliff does serve dairy products in the shape of ice-cream and creamers for coffee. This is rather a desecration of that poor sacred cow, who is exploited for its exudate, is it not?

Apart from this notable lapse, there is an admirable respect for the cow that pervades the restaurant and its menu. There are usually about thirty vegan tapas on offer. The ones we sampled were extraordinary--Korean Tofu Cutlets, the Shredded Tofu Spa Salad, and Curried Steamed Broccoli. The Hero Sandwich that we had as a main course --Roasted Black Olive Seitan, with molten vegan Mozzarella --was so good that we had to stifle a shout of jubilation. Fact is: Cliff's Hero sandwiches and pastries are so sought-after that he retails them to other snackeries around the city--like the one in the cafe at the Angelika Cinema.]

While we munched our Heroes, amid the warm, rouge tints of the interior decor, we sipped one of Cliff's frozen smoothies, which he calls Gym Body (bananas, toasted almonds, cinnamon, flax oil and apple juice). This was so satisfying that we could easily have made a meal of it.

For dessert we inhaled Cliff's famous Velvet Triple Chocolate Brownie with a side scoop of organic vegan Raspberry Ice-Cream. Cliff, [excuse the bad pun], we will be dropping over quite often, (especially if S. C. becomes 100% vegan).

• On a recent visit, we were delighted to learn that Sacred Chow has gone completely vegan! Did our caustic review have anything to do with their eliminating the mammary secretions from their meun? We fervently hope so! Kudos to Cliff.

'sNICE [v] $

Self service
Sandwiches, salads, baked goods
All cards
Beer & wine

45 8th Avenue
at 4th Street
212-645-0310
daily 7:30am-10pm

'sWonderful, 'sMarvelous, 'sNice? You'll surely agree that this coffee shop-cum-bistro deserves a loftier superlative than merely nice. Really, the food is nothing short of 'sMarvelous! That was our original evaluation of 'sNice during the first three years of its existence. Now, we're chagrined to report that, we've detected a dropoff in quality, which seems to have coincided with sNice's expansion into Park Slope, Brooklyn. Gone are the board games, children's toys, the Fizzi waters, and the vivid-tasting wraps that we used to adore. We've taken a number of our friends there over the past year. To a person, they've complained that the smoothies, the wraps and the clumps of salad served with them are insipid-tasting and monotonous. "The wraps smack of a doughy blandness with a sameness of flavor," said they. We are reluctantly forced to concur. Perhaps most off-putting of all, though, is the owner's attitude towards veganism, which is one of thinly disguised hostility. When asked if he would ever remove the honey, milk, Brie Cheese, Cream Cheese, Gorgonzola Cheese, Bleu Cheese, Goat Cheese, Mozzarella Cheese, Swiss Cheese, Parmesan Cheese, [Hey! Eight varieties of cheese on the menu! Is this a veg. bistro or a cheese shop?] and other mammary secretions from his menu, he bristled with indignation, and said "Never!"

'sOkay, 'sBland, 'sCheesy, but not 'sMarvelous, as it used to be. Let's hope that he may return to his former high standards, and go vegan!

See other locations under Greenwich Village and Brooklyn.

SOY & SAKE [v] $$

Full service
Japanese-pan Asian
All Cards
Sake bar
www.soyandsaake.com

47-49 Seventh Avenue South
bet.Bleecker / Morton Streets
212-255-2848
M-Sa 9am-9pm

Another first for New York: Soy 'N' Sake is New York'--if not the world's--first vegetarian sushi bar. Commonly, sushi contains fish; however, in this sushi bar, the sushi rolls are blessedly fin-, feather- and flesh-free. The place is owned by the same family who gave us those other landmarks of vegetarian gastronomy: VP-2 (Chinese} and Red Bamboo.(a fusion of pan-Asian and Southern Soul).

Seated comfortably at a table that looked onto 7th Avenue South, we started with the Mock Tuna (a rice wrapper enrobes avocado and marinated mock tuna chunks); We then had a Lettuce Wrap (a tender leaf of lettuce wraps a mixture of string beans, jicamas, carrots, grilled tofu, and rice-noodles served with a side of vegan hoisin sauce). The portions were so generous and so artfully prepared that we felt fully satisfied after downing the wrap and roll. Consequently, we decided to call it an evening after sharing one more sushi roll—the Hawaiian Roll (a sweetish tasting combination of banana chunks and Asian pear. enrobed in a wrapper of thin rice dough, and sliced into thin rounds).

Before leaving, we cast a wistful glance at the menu, feeling a pang of regret that we would never be able to taste any of the other delectable dishes. Towards the end of the meal, we had got up to explore the interior of the restaurant when we noticed something that troubled us deeply, and made us vow that as ethical vegans we could not, in good conscience, return to eat here. The full bar--where a variety of sakes and other alcoholic drinks are dispensed--is walled off by a floor-to-ceiling aquarium. It is painfully ironic that while the sushi contains no fish, the aquarium in the sushi bar not only imprisons fish, but exploits them for gaudy visual effects
• Recently friends had told us that the owners of Soy & Sake had bowed to pressure from our readers and had got rid of the fish tank. So we dropped by to inspect the situation for ourselves. Sure enough, we were told that the owner had given the fish to a fish sanctuary; however within a few months of our revisiting, they refilled the tank and re-stocked it with fish. So ethical vegetarians and vegans should protest.

TAIM [v] $

Counter service
Kosher Israeli falafel shack
All cards
No alcohol
www.taimnyc.com

222 Waverly Place
at 7th Avenue
212-691-1287
M-Su 11am-10:30pm

According to our researches, the first bona fide vegetarian Israeli falafel shack in NYC is this diminutive Greenwich Village spot called Taim. Since it was opened by Einat Admony, Taim's lady chef, two years ago, a number of others have sprung up, apparently, in imitation. Hummus Place on MacDougal Street and Moaz on Union Square East. Curiously enough, none of the owners of these ovo-lacto vegetarian falafel shacks is a vegetarian. They purvey vegetarian food simply because it is more expedient, more healthful, and hygienic to do so.

"Taim," which means delicious in Hebrew, is aptly named. "Taim" was practically every dish we tried here. We particularly relished the Falafel Sandwich. A pita pocket was filled with our choice of Green, Red or Harissa falafel balls and presented to us with side dishes of Israeli salad, pickled green cabbage, and tahini. The pickled carrot and beet salads were pleasingly tart and tasty. We also savored the Sabich (a pita sandwich of fried eggplant, slathered with pickles, onions, tahini and two types of hot sauce. The Sabich was invented by the Lord Sandwich of Israel-- Oved, a one-name-only denizen of the Tel Aviv suburb, Givatayim. It has since become the most popular hand-held food item in Israel. However, before ordering the Sabich, it is important to tell the chef to hold the eggs, because for some strange reason, a chick embryo is felt to be an obligatory ingredient in this dish.

We really liked their home-made French fries that we would rank second only to those of of FoodSwings in Williamsburg. We tossed off a delicious Strawberry-Raspberry-Thai-Basil smoothie, and a Ginger-Mint lemonade, which could make this place one of the city's better juice bars, were it not drenched in milk. However, they use whole and skim milk in their smoothies, so vegans should ask that the blender be washed, before making a non-dairy smoothie, to expel any caseous residues/ The service staff will honor your request with alacrity.

VEGETARIAN'S PARADISE-2 $$ 👍

Full service
Chinese
$4.95-12.95 (AE,MC,V)
No alcohol

140 / 144 West 4th Street
bet. Sixth Ave/ MacDougal Street
212-260-7130/7141
M-Th 12pm-11pm, F-Sa 12pm-12am

We know, you've long since given up ordering Peking Spare Ribs, Sweet and Pungent Pork and Squid in Black Bean Sauce. Do it anyway. The meaty names just help identify traditional Chinese dishes that VP's Buddhist chefs prepare exclusively without animal products (using soy, wheat, and arrowroot substitutes). The food is authentic and reasonably priced, served in a modern, sleek restaurant . One of the best of this type of place.

👍 Indicates we especially recommend this restaurant for the quality of the food

EAST VILLAGE
(Houston to East 14th Street, Fifth Avenue to the East River)

ANGELICA KITCHEN [ve] **$$** 👍

Full service
Organic
No cards
No alcohol

300 E 12th Street
at Second Avenue
212-228-2909
daily 11:30am-10:30pm

Hands down one of the best vegan restaurants anywhere. For 25 years Angelica Kitchen has set the standard for fresh organic fare with a conscience.

Each day there are two very special, always new, special entrees such as "Here Today-- Gone Tamale'" (Festive tamales made with Iroquois white corn masa and roasted home-made seitan, chipotle and ancho chili peppers, all wrapped in a corn husk served with tomato-cilantro salsa, over a baby lima bean sauce, with baby lettuces and steamed local asparagus). Or try the norimake rolls with grilled tempeh, home-made pickled carrots and brown rice; like sushi, they're rolled in nori seaweed .

For those who wish to try Angelica Kitchen's tasty dishes at home, the Angelica Home Kitchen Cookbook by Leslie McEachern (the owner) is for sale in the restaurant. It includes over 100 recipes from the menu archives that have been specially formulated for the home cook. The book also sets forth Leslie's philosophy and principles for running a socially conscious business, and it features profiles of the farmers and artisans who provide the restaurant with the ingredients for their delicious fare.

Angelica's is a dessertatarian's delight. We swooned over the rhubarb layer cake with strawberry frosting and the coconut flan with pineapple salsa was unforgettable. Consistently fresh, flavorful and satisfying, the whole vital menu proves why the outstanding reputation of Angelica Kitchen is so richly deserved Take-out next door.

BEYOND SUSHI [ve] **$** 👍

Counter Service
Vegan kosher sushi
All cards
No alcohol
www. BeyondSushiNYC.Com

229 East 14th Street
bet. 2nd/ 3rd Avenues
646-861-2889
Su- W 11:30am-10pm
Th-Sa 11:30am-11pm

Isn't it ironic that a young Jewish guy from Morocco should be so adept at making vegan sushi that his Japanese clients, which are legion, should implore him to open a branch of his vegan *sushiya* in Tokyo? Yet that is exactly what happens, (almost on a weekly basis)--to Guy Vaknin.

While working for his family's Brooklyn-based kosher catering business, Esprit Events, he hit upon the idea of making exclusively vegetarian sushi, and found that he had a knack for producing it.

Since NYC is a propitious place for launching single item vegan food restaurants a la Dun-Well Doughnuts, New York Dosas, Moshe's Falafel-- Guy decided to take a leaf from their book and become the vegan sushi guy.

When he first opened Beyond Sushi, it wasn't entirely vegan. He spiked some of his rolls with eggs, and used honey in sauces, but such was the outcry from the vegan community, that he bowed to the pressure, and after being open for only a few weeks, he turned vegetarian, and started serving 100% vegan sushi.

We particularly enjoyed the Spicy Mango roll, which contains a base of Chinese forbidden black rice; and is filled with avocado, mango, cucumber, and spicy vegetables. It was served with a Toasted Cayenne Sauce.

We also highly recommend the rice paper wraps. Our favorite, and the most popular, is the Nutty Buddy. It is filled with buckwheat noodles; crushed peanuts; cilantro; jalapeno peanut butter; avocado; sesame oil; baked tofu, and romaine. It was served with a Sweet Miso Sauce. The sushi at Beyond Sushi--brightly bejeweled with fruits and vegetables--is as eye-catching as it is delicious!

See other location at Midtown West.

CAFE VIVA [A.K.A. VIVA HERBAL PIZZERIA] [v] $

Counter service
Italian, organic, kosher
All cards
No alcohol

179 Second Avenue
bet. 11th / 12th Streets
212-420-8801
daily 11am-11pm
Sa-Su 11am-12am

See /Description under Upper West Side

CARAVAN OF DREAMS [ve] $$$ 👍

Full service
International organic, kosher
V,MC
Full bar, organic beer & wine
www.caravanofdreams.net/

405 East 6th Street
bet. First Ave/Avenue A
212-254-1613
M,Su 11am-11pm, Sa 11am-12am
Sa,,Su brunch 11am-5pm

Organic vegetarian food in a hippy atmosphere of long hair, mix and match furniture and live music almost every night. Quite relaxing during non-peak hours. No dairy is used; a few years ago, Caravan went completely vegan. Black bean chili, grilled polenta, African spinach stew over rice, pasta, burritos, quesadilla, wild rice and cremini risotto croquettes, large salads, sandwiches, "greens of the day." A pleasure. Recently Caravan has begun serving raw-food entrees every day. It also serves a range of raw soups and desserts. Their avocado coconut soup is simply ravishing! And their raw raspberry cake bears comparison with any baked cake in town. Every night, their new raw chef creates live food specials that rotate every week. We enjoyed the Taco Salad, the Live Mock Meat Balls, the Live Nachos, and the Live Sandwich. Obviously Caravan's Dreams have come to life.

DIRT CANDY $$$ 👍

Full service
Vegetarian haute cuisine
All major cards
Wine
www.dirtcandynyc.com

430 East 9th Street
bet. First/ A Avenues
212-228-7732
T-Sa 5:30pm-11pm

Casting about for a euphemistic name for her restaurant that didn't feature the highly charged "V" word, Amanda Cohen, the owner-chef, hit upon "Dirt Candy." as a synonym for vegetables. At the foot of her menu, she has written this epigraph: "Made of little more than water and sunlight, vegetables are candy from the dirt. We want you to relax, have fun and be surprised at how good they can be." For those who want to learn more about Amanda's food philosophy, and culinary adventures, read *Dirt Candy: A Cookbook*, (2012), which is written partially in graphic novel format.

The food here is ovo-lacto vegetarian; so it's mandatory for vegans to declare themselves at the start of the meal or, preferably, when making reservations. Reservations are a must because the room holds only 19 diners who sit cheek by jowl. Crammed into this same small room, is a mini-bathroom and a tmicro-kitchen where food is prepared, orders are plated, and dishes are washed and dried.

Despite the close quarters, Dirt Candy is a fitting showcase for Amanda's talents, not only as a creative chef but also as a restaurant manager. She doesn't just stir the pot and point a spatula at uniformed flunkies; she waits on tables, she cooks, and she even washes dishes in a hyperkinetic blur of energy that is as enthralling to watch as the food is to eat.

Such an air of *bonhommi*e pervades the room that we chatted amiably with the diners to our left and right, as if we were all seated at a communal table. Topic A was the food and how *exquise* it was. Each course evoked oooh's and aaah's. We started with peppery Jalapeno Hush Puppies which were served with an ambrosial tasting maple vegan spread. For teetotalers, like us, the waitress poured an endless flow of non-alcoholic Riesling wine [Navarro Vineyards] from California. Next, we had the Mixed Green Salad with mock cheese croutons and Candied Grapefruit Pops. For the main course, we had The Crispy Tofu in Green Ragout, which consisted of grilled tofu topped with a bundle of micro-greens and a-swim in a sauce made from chopped Brussels sprouts and vivid, crunchy vegetables. Having cheffed at rawfoods restaurants like Pure Food and Wine under Matthew "Everyday Raw" Kenney, Amanda, has gained the insight that vegetables are more flavorful and colorful when they are slightly undercooked. For dessert, Amanda served us a layered vegan ice cream bar that--taken with all the other wondrous dishes of Amanda's devising--has given us a permanent sweet tooth for Dirt Candy

GINGER SNAPS ORGANIC[ve] *$$* 👍

Full service
Vegan organic raw food
Visa, Master Card
No alcohol
www. Ginbersnapsorganic.com

130 East Seventh Street
bet. 1st & A Avenues
212-533-9939
M-F 11am-11pm
Sa-Su 12pm-11pm

This organic raw food café is named after its owner, Jamie "Ginger Snaps" Graber, 'a red head with attitude," as she humorously describes herself. She acquired her raw knowledge at Live-Live and Organic in New York, and Euphoria Loves RAWvolution in Santa Monica.

Currently presiding over the stove-less Ginger Snaps Organic kitchen is Chef William, a protégé of Scott Weingard, formerly the head chef at Pure Food and Wine. Chef William's creations are certainly worthy of his mentor.

We particularly relished his Reuben Wrap (home-made sauerkraut, sun-dried tomatoes, romaine lettuce, and Russian dressing), his Nori Wrap, which was filled with avocado, red bell pepper, cucumbers, rice made from cauliflower, and seasoned with wasabi sauce; his Flatbread Pizza (walnut-hemp-seed crust, sun-dried tomatoes, garlic, nutritional yeast, and Brazil nut cheese); his Caesar Salad (lettuce, broccoli sprouts, sunflower seeds, caper berries, chick-pea miso); and for dessert—his Chia Seed Pudding (plumped chia seeds, almond milk, and palm sugar)--much the best pudding we've ever tasted.

"Ginger Snaps" Jamie, pointed out to us that the raw cuisine at Ginger Snaps Organic is seed-based rather than nut-based, so it is not so heavy or calorfic as that of other raw food restaurants. One of the great things about Ginger Snaps Organic is that it is open so late; indeed, one may eat healthful and delicious raw vegan organic cuisine here beyond the stroke of midnight.

HUMMUS PLACE [v] *$*

Full Service
Israeli vegetarian, kosher
All cards
Wine & Beer

109 St. Marks Place
bet. 1st & A Avenues
212-529-9198
Su-Th 11am-12am
Fr-Sa 11am-2am

See description under Greenwich Village, and other location under Upper West Side.

JIVAMUKTEA CAFE [ve] *$$* 👍

Counter Service
Global vegan organic
All cards

841 Broadway (2nd Fl.)
bet. 13th/ 14th Streets
212-353-0214
M-F 11am-9pm

Overlooking the hubbub of Broadway in a spacious, airy setting, with an azure ceiling, antique chandeliers. and soaring stained glass windows, the new JivamukTea Café is housed inside the Jivamukti Yoga Center, which, from an ethical standpoint, is the best school of yoga in the city.

Unlike most yoga ashrams that give short shrift to *ahimsa,* which is the first precept of all classical yoga systems. it is clear that Jivamukti's founders, Sharon Gannon and David Life, uphold the view of Patanjali that if one is to advance spiritually in yoga one must eat non-violent food. In fact, in a recent interview, Sharon Gannon said," Veganism is essential to the practice of yoga, where you do not exploit animals for any purpose. Patanjali in the *Yoga Sutras,* gives *ahimsa* (non-harming of others) as the primary means to enlightenment." To that end, Sharon Gannon has created a menu that is conducive to attaining the higher states of yogic consciousness—and to having a transcendent dining experience.

This JivamukTea Café is figuratively a reincarnation of the first JivamukTea Cafe, which was managed by star chef Matthew Kenney, and went defunct not long after it opened. However, this new incarnation promises to have more staying power because it is that much better than its predecessor, which tried too hard to be trendy. Overseen by new General Manager, Kevin Archer, this one's recipes come from co-founder Sharon Gannon's home kitchen, so they have a familial, home-style air to them.

We tried their most popular sandwich, the Grilled Portobello Panino (portabella mushroom, sweet onions, nutritional yeast, chimchurri sauce on grilled sourdough). Yummy! Then we proceeded to have the Montana Salad, which contains seasonal vegetables, lettuce, cucumbers, black beans, quinoa, sprouts grown on the premises--all of it suffused with a turmeric-tahini dressing. Heavenly! To wash it down, we chugged a 3rd Eye Smoothie (acai, coconut water, banana, and organic vanilla extract). Ambrosial! For dessert, we had the Walnut Cake and the oversized Chocolate Chip Cookie that had just been plucked from the oven--with the result that the chips were still gooey and the dough was still soft and friable. Celestial! It was a vegan Toll House Cookie raised to a higher order of cookie. After dessert, as we watched the sunlight shimmering through the stained glass, we sipped, meditatively two generous cups of Love Blend Tea, a black tea with subtle chocolate overtones.

In spite of all the delicious food we had eaten, we seemed to float on air as we left the café, mumbling a *sotto voce* M-m-m-m-m mingled with Om-m-m-m-m-m.

JUICE PRESS, THE [v] $$ 👍

Counter service
Organic Juices and raw food
All Cards
No alcohol

201 East 10th Street
bet. 2nd /1st Avenues/
212-777-0034
    daily 8am-10pm

JUICE PRESS, THE [v] $$ 👍

Counter service
Organic Juices and raw food

279 East 10th Street
bet. 1st /A Avenues/

All Cards
No alcohol

212-777-0034
daily 8am-10pm

JUICE PRESS, THE [v] **$$**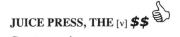

Counter service
Organic Juices and raw food
All Cards
No alcohol
Thejuicepressonline.com

70 East 1st Street
bet. 1st / 2nd Avenues/
212-777-0034
daily 8am-10pm

When he was a much younger man, Marcus Antebi, the founder of The Juice Press, worked with his father in the antiques business. Ironically enough, now that he is approaching middle age, he's in the rejuvenation business. He takes prematurely antique and wizened younger folk, and by putting them on a vegan raw food diet--interspersed with juice cleanses--he reinvigorates them in body as well as in spirit

With the muscular physique and the high verve of the Muay Thai kick-boxer that he is, Marcus is the best advertisement for his vegan rawfoodist lifestyle. Recently a reporter from the New York Times Style section put herself under Marcus's tutelage and afterwards felt transfigured. On Day 10 of her program, she was ecstatic over losing 11 pounds. and has become a confessed addict of the vegan raw foods and juice elixirs that helped her shed her surplus poundage—such as "Complete Source"(carrot, celery, spinach, parsley). The juice blends, are hydraulically expressed from organic fruits and vegetables by powerful Norwalk Juicers,. [Norwalk Juicers--the most efficient juicers on the market—are used because they minimize nutrient and enzyme loss.]

Ideally, Marcus tells us, the juice cleanses are a preparation for embarking on a high raw vegan diet. Marcus's mentor, Dr. Fred Bisci , who is in his early 80s , but could pass for a youthful 50, has been extolling the virtues of a raw food vegan diet for more than 40 years. His motto is "It's not what you put into your body, but what you leave out."

What we put into our body, however, was not only delicious, but also energizing and uplifting. Which is seldom one's condition after a cooked meal. It's important to emphasize that, despite its name, The Juice Press, serves up some of the tastiest and most healthful solid food in town. We started with the Marinated Kale Salad (marinated kale, steeped in a lime dressing, and nutritional yeast is topped with nori, tomato, avocado, and sprouts.) Next we had their Ravioli (raw sliced turnips are filled with homemade vegan cashew cheese, garnished with black sesame seeds, and served with homemade raw pesto.) For dessert, we ate their raw Acai Nut Mix (raw organic acai berry, buckwheat, sunflower, walnuts, flax, almonds, coconut oil, vanilla, cacao, blueberry).

The Juice Press is so successful that it has already expanded to three branches within the space of a year. Rawfoodism and Norwalk cold pressed juices seem to be riding the crest of a wave that is engulfing (and cleansing) the city.

LAN CAFE [v] **$**

Full service
Vietnamese
Cash only
Beer & wine

342 East 6th Street
bet. 1st/ 2nd Avenue
212-228-8325
Tu-Su 2pm-11pm

Last summer, we sampled vegan dishes in some Vietnamese restaurants in Hawaii--where there is a large settlement of Vietnamese folk, but, alas, no vegan Vietnamese restaurants. Admittedly, the food was very good, but the food at Lan Cafe--New York's first vegetarian Vietnamese restaurant--surpasses that of the best in Honolulu. Perhaps it's because the co-owner/chef --Cao Ky and his wife Lan--are devout Mahayana Buddhists and therefore are ethical vegans. Hence, the food, except for the condensed milk coffee creamer, is cruelty-free , and, on our many visits, the pure, unalloyed flavors of this essentially Buddhist Vietnamese cuisine shone forth.

In fact, the food at Lan Cafe is so exquisite, that we played a little parlor game--we challenged each other to find a dish on the menu that we didn't like. After repeated visits, we exhausted the menu without being able to find a dish that we didn't adore. All are extraordinary. At Lan Cafe, we must speak of the extraordinary among extraordinaries. These are the best vegan eats of the East!

We recommend that you start with the classic Vietnamese dish --a staple on the menus of restaurants in Saigon--Green Papaya Salad with Mock Shrimp. Follow this with Pho--another classic Vietnamese dish. A capacious bowl is filled with a healthy serving of vegetable broth aswim with long rice noodles, and vegetarian beef. On the side are served bean sprouts and basil leaves. At intervals, these are to be added to the Pho. The flavors, of both the Green Papaya Salad and the Pho, were stupendous!

Fact is: Frank, the manager, had warned us that the Pho at Lan Cafe is so filling that there is scant room for anything else. He was right. We wanted to try the Curried Lemon Grass Seitan, and the Baguettes with Vegetarian Sausage and the one with Vegetarian Mock Ham (an incongruous Gallicism here that is doubtless the legacy of the French colonial occupation of Vietnam, as is the name of that glorious soup, pho, which is a corruption of the French word for fire *feu*.)--but we had to postpone those gustatory sensations for our next visit. Our only puzzlement was why was it so easy to find a table here? By rights, there should be lines of vegan gourmets winding around the block.

How did the Lan Cafe get its name. In Vietnamese the word "lan" means "orchid." "Orchidaceous" would aptly describe the cuisine--exotic, eye-filling, and drop-dead delicious!

LULA"S SWEET APOTHECARY [ve] $

	516 East 6th Street
Counter service	bet. Avenues A & B
Gourment vegan ice-cream	646-912-4549
No cards	Su, Tu, W 3pm-10pm
No alcohol	Th,F, Sa 3pm-11:30pm
www.lulasweet.com	

Derek and Blythe, are the owners of New York's first vegan ice-cream parlor. They earned their stripes in Philadelphia where for two years they operated a food truck called Viva Las Vegans on the campus of Drexel University. While plying their trade on the Drexel campus, they conceived the bright idea of opening a vegan ice-cream parlor in NYC. Undaunted, they sold Viva Las Vegans; moved to New York City; and, in October, 2008, opened Lula's which is named for Blythe's niece. The rest is vegan history, or should we say her-story?

Half-Vietnamese, and all-American, Blythe is an alumna of the elite Mt. Holyoke College in Massachusetts. Her business partner, Derek, is from Ireland and speaks with an engaging brogue. An indefatigable worker, with the skills (and muscles) of a cabinet-maker, Derek built the oak paneled interior that recalls an old-time ice-cream parlor, vintage 1947.

Think of Lula's then as an old-fashioned drugstore-cum-soda fountain without the drugstore, (and the drugstore cowboys). It evokes the sort of place that gave us the term "soda jerk" and; and where Pemberton invented the recipe for Coca-Cola; and where movie stars like Lana Turner were "discovered." It displays apothecary jars stuffed with sweets, and dispenses all the old soda-fountain treats--eggless egg-creams, banana splits, and. of course, the immortal sundae.

The ice-creams are nut-, water-, and soy-based of which a high preponderance are nut-based. Last time we were there, Blythe and Derek--who are constantly experimenting with new flavors-- had just contrived chocolate malt and vanilla malt flavors; they were so delicious that we hope they'll become staples. Some of our other favorites include coconut fudge; peanut-butter fudge; cake-batter soft serve twist; and cinnamon-pecan.

MAOZ III [v] $

Counter service
Israeli falafel shack, kosher
All Cards
No alcohol
www.maozusa.com

59 East 8th Street
bet. Broadway/ University Place
212-420-5999
daily 11am-12am

See description under Midtown East and other location under Upper West Side.

PEACEFOOD CAFÉ- DOWNTOWN [ve] $$

41 East 11th Street
at University Place
212-979-2288
M-Su 10am-10pm

Full service
Vegan world cuisine
All cards
No alcohol

World-class interior designer, Peter Lu, who has designed the inside of many a swanky restaurant, has surpassed himself by creating the most striking restaurant interior in NYC. Warm, and cozy, yet elegant, it is said to replicate his own living room. It's the pluprefect place for consuming the restaurants prize-winning dishes such as The Other Caesar, Dumplings, Chick-Pea Fries, Raw Lasagna, Roasted Potato Pizza, et al. In fact, the sparkling ambience bids fair to ourshine its resplendent up-town branch on 82nd Street and Amsterdam Avenue! The kitchen is many times the size of the flagship branch, enabling Eric Yu to make the most eleborate and delicious veggie burger in town—which we call the Eric Burger, after the former supreme court chief justice, because it truly is supreme! Both Peter Lu and his partner Eric Yu gave up high-flying careers in the arts and design world to run their two restaurants because they are utterly dedicated to furthering the cause of world peace through food activism—Peacefood activism.

See other location at Upper West Side

POMMES FRITES [v] $

123 Second Avenue
bet. Seventh/ Eighth Streets
212-674-1234
daily 11:30am-Midnight

Counter Service
Belgian French fries
No cards
No alcohol

Studies have shown that people go to burger joints mainly for the French fries. With the opening of Pommes Frites and its opposite number, B. Frites at 1657 Broadway, it's now possible for vegetarians to dine on French Fries without having to make a clandestine visit to the Golden Arches. In Belgium, the *maison de pommes frites* is a thriving concern. So some enterprising Americans have imported the idea to New York and judging from the lines that form up at Pommes Frites and B. Frites, it's really taking hold. The fries at Pommes Frites are double cooked in the Belgian manner, and are served with a range of tasty sauces. For vegans, it's necessary to inquire about the composition of the sauces as some may contain mayonnaise and other objectionable ingredients. We managed quite nicely with a double cone of fries that we dipped alternately in etchup and mustard, which are on the house; the other sauces are fifty cents extra.

PUKK [v] $$

Full service
Thai vegetarian
All cards
Beer, wine, champagne
www.pukknyc.com

75 First Avenue
bet. 4th/ 5th Streets
212-253-2742
daily 11:30am-11pm

A four-letter word in Thai that means "vegetable," Pukk is an apt name for this all-vegetarian Thai restaurant. Imaginatively designed to make maximum use of the rather cramped dining spaces, Pukk is a model of elegant compression. But the menu enables one to dine spaciously on delicious Thai vegetarian fare. It's not quite vegan here because, inexplicably they serve eggs?!!!? So vegans should inquire about eggs in the noodles, in the pastries, in the soups, and sauces, etc. But everything else is impeccably plant-based. In fact, the Pukksters thoughtfully provide soy milk for tea, coffee, and smoothies. For starters, try the Tom Yum Soup, a yummy soup that is aswim with chunks of spiced tofu, mushrooms, scallions and cilantro; then try the Curry Thai Pancake, a flaky crepe served in a piquant curry sauce. Follow this with the Faux Salmon; or, if you prefer to avoid faux meats, try the tofu dishes--such as Stuffed Tofu, or the Son-in-Law Tofu--at which Thai chefs excel. If there is a rawfooder in your midst, then he or she will be certain to enjoy the All Green Salad, which layers fresh vegetables on a mound of fresh greens. It is nattily and nuttily dressed with a splash of spicy peanut sauce.

Dessert here is a bit of an anticlimax after the crescendo of flavors leading up to it. So we recommend ambling over to Caravan of Dreams, or Babycakes for a truly scrumptious dessert. Although the food here is not so good as that of the Thai vegan restaurant in Montreal called Chu Chai, which for our money is one of the best vegan restaurant in the world, it is good enough, because of its sheer exoticism, to be one of the better vegetarian restaurants in New York

QUINTESSENCE [ve] $$$

Full Service
Raw food vegetarian, organic
All cards
No alcohol
www.raw-q.com

263 East 10th Street
bet. 1st Avenue/ Avenue A
646-654-1823
daily 11:am-11pm

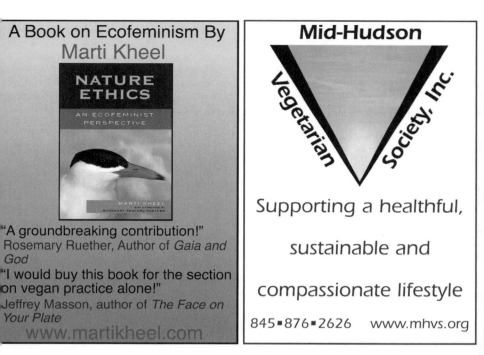
For skeptics who think that raw food is a penitential diet of roots, shoots and fruits, Tolentin and her business partner Dan Hoyt, who have been strict rawfoodists for four years, are on a mission to show people that rawfood can be as toothsome as it is nutritious. So admirably have they succeeded that you'd swear that some of the dishes are cooked. Ironically, the mark of a good raw food dish is that it tastes as if it's been cooked. This is certainly true of the Sun Burger, a hearty patty made of sunflower and flaxseed meal mixed with chopped celery, onions, red pepper and herbs dehydrated to a burger consistency and served between slices of dehydrated bread. {The temperature of the dehydrator in which the breads are baked must never rise above an enzyme-killing 120 degrees). Another entree, the Caribbean Nut Meatballs which are served in an aromatic, zesty pineapple-tomato sauce also earns the accolade: "Tastes as if it's been cooked." The Coconut Cream Pie and the Pecan Pie are the quintessence of desserts, fired or unfired, anywhere in the city.

• We were gratified to learn that Quintessence is now 100 percent organic and vegan. When they first opened, we lobbied for them to stop using honey in their dishes, and we like to think that we have played a small role in their going completely vegan. Credit to chef Dan!

'sNICE III [v] $

150 Sullivan Street
bet. Prince/ Houston
212-253-5405
M-F 7:30am-10pm
Sa-Su 8am-10pm

Self service
Sandwiches, salads, baked goods
All cards
Beer & wine

See description under Greenwich Village, and other location under Brooklyn

SUSTAINABLE NYC [v] $ 👍

139 Avenue A
at Ninth Street
212-254-5400
M-F 8am-8pm
Sa, Su 9am-8pm

Counter service
International
No credit cards
No alcohol
Sustainable-nyc.com

Now customers who wish to lessen their carbon footprint by buying Sustainable New York City's green products--such as biodegradable beauty products; solar backpacks; and chargers for i-pods and blackberries; bio-degradable home cleaning products; recycled stationery, etc.—now, they can shrink their carbon footprint even further by eating at SNYC's in-store café--the vegetarian edition of Ciao for Now.

Ciao for Now, (pun intended) is a family-run restaurant that was started by Amy and Kevin Miceli in 2001. The main location is at 523 East 12th Street between Avenues A and B. Don't look for a review of Ciao For Now in *The Vegan Guide to New York City*, however; because--at its main location and at its other satellite location at 107 W. 10th Street—ruefully, it's not vegetarian.

However, genuflecting to the green ethos of SNYC, Ciao for Now has custom designed a vegetarian menu for its owner, Dominique. We recently chowed at CFN in SNYC starting with the Asian Chop: (Marinated tofu, tarmari almonds, edamame, sprouts, and carrots in a sesame dressing). This is *una bella insalata*! We followed this with a Hummus Sandwich (served on 9-grain bread and filled with carrots, red pepper, sprouts and lettuce). Bravo!

For dessert, we had a tranche of chocolate vegan cake and a Double Chocolate Vegan Espresso Cookie. To wash down the cake and cookie, we sipped a vegan cappuccino (made with fair-trade Ink coffee) that was so savory and smooth that we had doubles on it. In a word, the vegetarian edition of Ciao for Now is a perfect fit for Sustainable NYC.

👍 Indicates we especially recommend this restaurant for the quality of the food

TABLE VERTE $$$ 👍

Full service
Vegetarian French bistro cuisine
Amex only
Wine & beer
www.tablevertenyc.com

127 East 7th Street
bet. First/ A Avenues
212-539-023`
Su-Th 5pm-10pm
F-Sa 5pm-11pm

The first vegetarian French restaurant in New York City, Table Verte is making culinary history even as we write this. Chef Ken, who received his culinary education at the French Culinary Institute in Soho (at the corner of Broadway and Grand Streets) wears *la tocque verte* with authority here. He honed his skills in Gallic cooking by working at a Michelin one-star restaurant in Nancy, France. Since then, he had worked in restaurants all over the US--until one day he had his vegetarian epiphany. It happened while he was working--in of all places—a steak house! Terminally bored with preparing and eating the grey slabs of dead flesh that he was charged with making palatable--by perfuming them with recherche sauces--he decided to take the vow of vegetables.

Such is Chef Ken's artistry with vegetables, that he prides himself on not having to rely on mock meats to beef up his menu. You'll not find tofu or tempeh, or seitan here. (Albeit, soy milk is available as a coffee creamer.) Instead, vegetables are accorded the respect that they deserve. At Table Verte vegetables occupy center stage. We started with *Haricots Verts*, which we figured would be a test of Ken's talents. Lightly sautéed with garlic and parsley, they passed our taste test with flying tri-colors. We then had the *Assiete de Crudites*, which is a plate comprising three healthy dollops of three different salads: Carrots and Raisins; Mushroom Caponata, and Beets with Horseradish. Each salad was distinctive and flavorful. We then ordered the seasonal special, which turned out to be Roast Brussels Sprouts with Strawberries, an improbable combination that worked. We still had room for another dish; so we plumped for the *Fennel & Petit Onion Confit* which consisted of Rosemary polenta, roasted peppers and tomato sauce. Among the dishes that we ordered this was our favorite—so many different taste sensations concentrated in one dish. It was a culinary tour de force. We concluded our meal with *Annana Epice roti couli de Mures* (Roast smoked chipotle-spiced pineapple with a touch of sea salt, coconut sorbet and a blackberry sauce.) A couple at a nearby table noticed what we were having and promptly ordered this dessert for themselves. They and we were not disappointed. The dessert like all the other dishes at Table Verte that we ate with gusto—*C'etait magnifique!*

SOHO
(Canal Street to Houston Street)

BABYCAKES [ve] **$**

Counter service
Vegan baked goods
All cards
No alcohol
www.babycakesnyc.com

248 Broome Street
bet. Orchard/ Ludlow Streets
212-677-5047
Tu-Th 10am-10pm
F 10am-10pm
Su-M 10am-8pm

Although the art-deco, retro interior evokes a roadside diner from the 1920's, unless you're a dessertatarian--as we are--then it's not really possible to have a meal here; however, if you have an overdeveloped sweet tooth--as we do--then you could have a chocolate chip cookie as an appetizer, a carrot cupcake as a main course with some extra frosting on the side [It's $1.50 for a side order of frosting.]--and a slice of pound cake for dessert. You could wash it down with a cup of shade-grown, fair-trade Gorilla coffee, as we did.

Here's a rich irony--the owner, Erin McKenna, is not a vegetarian, but she is scrupulous about not using eggs, or dairy. Instead of honey, she uses stevia and agave nectar --whereas, the techno-pop star Moby, who is a militant vegan, serves eggs, honey and dairy products at his restaurant, Teany, which is only a few blocks away.

Let's face it, there are a lot of excellent vegan and vegetarian restaurants in New York that have execrable desserts--Pukk, Madras Cafe, Vegetarian Dim Sum House, to list but a few. So, have your dinner at Madras Cafe; then saunter over to Babycakes for some sweet, sweet babycakes for dessert. Our current favorites (as of 2010) are the Cinnamon Toastie, plus their new doughnuts—glazed, chocolate, sprinkles and coconut.

HUMMUS SHOP, THE [v] **$**

Counter Service
Israeli vegetarian, kosher
All cards
Wine & Beer

101 Ludlow Street
at Delancey Street
212-260-0661
Su-Th 10am-11pm
Fr-Sa 10am-4am

Yet another in New York's growing number of hummus shacks. We liked their Moroccan Carrot Salad and the Hummus Mushroom. Like the other hummus places in the city, it is not vegan. In fact this one is overly ovo-lacto.

Do You Have A Passion
for Sharing the Vegan Message?

Earn Certification as a
Vegan Lifestyle Coach and Educator (VLCE)

In this 5 day intensive LIVE and in person in fabulous NYC
you'll learn with **Main Street Vegan** author **Victoria Moran**
and faculty of Vegan Luminaries and Experts.
Plus exciting field trips!

www.mainstreetvegan.net/academy
212-289-1808

JUICE PRESS, THE [ve] $$ 👍

Counter service
Organic Juices and raw food
All Cards

156 Prince Street
West of Broadway (Soho)
212-777-0034

JUICE PRESS, THE [ve] $$ 👍

Counter service
Organic Juices and raw food
All Cards

107 Rivington Street
bet. Bet. Ludlow/ Essex Streets
212-777-0034

JUICE PRESS, THE [ve] $$ 👍

Counter service
Organic Juices and raw food
All Cards
No alcohol
Thejuicepressonline.com

250 Mott Street
bet. Prince/ Houston Streets
212-777-0034
daily 8am-10pm

For description see East Village, and other locations passim.

ORGANIC AVENUE [ve] $$ 👍

Self service
Organic raw food bar/boutique

156 Sullivan Street
bet. West Houston / Prince Street

ORGANIC AVENUE [ve] $$ 👍

Full service
Organic raw food boutiaue
All major cards
No alcohol
www.organicavenue.com

116 Suffolk Street
bet. Delancey/ Rivington Streets
212-358-0500
M-F 8am-8pm
Sa,Su 8am-10pm

Time was when Organic Avenue sold hemp clothing, organic lifestyle products, books, organic vegan snacks, as well as organic fruits and vegetables. They still do, but the raw organic fruits and vegetables have given way to organic raw fruit and vegetable juices and smoothies along with chef-crafted raw food dishes.

It was when founder-owner, Denise Mari met her husband Doug, an astute vegan businessman, that they started to focus intently on selling cold pressed organic raw juices, smoothies, and raw organic vegan prepared foods. The juices, smoothies, and foods were dispensed in containers and sold in refrigerator cases. In late 2010, they hired gourmet raw food chef, Peter Cerevoni-- who had trained under raw food chef Chad Sarno, of Vital Creations—to imbue OA's organic vegan raw food with his authority and culinary flair.

We quaffed a Blueberry Smoothie and followed it with a Portobello Sandwich. For dessert, we ate their Coco-Lime Pie. All were surpassingly yummy. Unusually, after such a heavy meal, we felt strangely lifted and energized.

While I browsed the raw food books, my companion tried on a pastel top, which was on sale for half price. At Organic Avenue, there is a juxtaposition of food, books, and clothing that gratified all our appetites save one. All in all, luncheon at OA was a thoroughly engaging way to wile away an afternoon.

See other locations passim.

PUNJAB [v] $
Counter service
Indian fast food
No cards
No alcohol

114 East First Street
at Avenue A
212-533-9048
daily 24 hours

This unprepossessing samosa shack is hard to find, but worth a look-in. It's located in the basement of a building on East First Street with an awning that is misleadingly labeled as a deli-grocery. Down the stairs, one spies Indian cabdrivers munching on samosas, rotis and other vegetarian delights. We mimicked them and ordered a Tikki (potato pancake) slathered with chickpeas and told the counterman that we wanted it without milk, cheese or ghee. Like everyone else in this bustling, cramped place--we ate it standing up. It went down very well.

In the refrigerated display case, there are other pre-cooked curry dishes that just need to be heated in the microwave to be revived. We tried the Curried Bitter Melon, and found it astringent but tasty. The fact that cabbies eat here is a good sign. Typically, cabbies seek out the most flavorful and frugal vegetarian food. So their presence is almost a guarantee of a satisfying meal, however hurried.

RAWLICIOUS [ve] $$

Full service   249 Centre Street
Vegan, organic, raw food   bet. Broome/ Grand Streets
All cards   212-226-5200
No alcohol   daily 11am-11pm
www. Rawlicioususa.com

Further proof that the raw food movement isn't peculiar to Los Angeles, or New York is the recent opening of Rawlicious, an upscale vegan, organic raw food restaurant that is actually one of a chain of such restaurants whose flagship is in Toronto, Canada. Its Toronto-based owners, Chelsea Clark, and Angus Crawford were persuaded to open a branch in NYC by a vegan New York physician and his son, who were impressed by the high quality and healthfulness of the food.

We were impressed by the generous portions and the vivid flavors of the food to say nothing of the posh décor and the gracious service. We highly recommend the raw pizzas, whose delicious toppings are changed every day. We adored the nut and seed flatbreads that were filled with cherry tomatoes and caramelized onions., but the Pad Thai with its spiralized zucchini noodles and cashew cheese fell really flat! We topped off our meals with a cinnabun and raw ice-cream. Predictably, we pronounced the entire meal from raw soup to nut-based ice-cream positively "rawlicious!"

TEANY [v] $

                                               90 Rivington Street
Full service   bet. Orchard/ Ludlow
International   212-475-9190
All cards)   W, Th, Su 10am-10pm
Beer & wine   F, Sa 10am-2am

Teany is a restaurant-cum-teahouse that was founded by the rock star Moby. Its name, Teany, stands for Tea New York, but it is also a pun, referring wryly to its diminutive size. It's teeny as well as teany. The portions, however, are ample. For instance the faux turkey club sandwich, which we adored, is big enough to feed two people; and the salads, the crostini, and the granola dishes are as generous as they are delicious. Along with the Club Sandwich, we recommend the Crostini. Thin toast ovals are served with four vegan spreads--Olive, White Bean, Artichoke and Herbed Soy Cheese. It's big of Teany that after you've dipped all your toast ovals in the pots of vegan spreads, Teany will freely replenish them.

Teany desserts are tremendous! We particularly liked the Tofu Chocolate Cheese Cake, and the Peanut Butter Chocolate cake, which are supplied to Teany by the Vegan Treats bakery. The eponymous tea menu is as extensive as any four star restaurant's wine list. Last time we were there, we savored the black tea called Golden Monkey,. but there are uncaffeinated herb teas as well. Sad to report: we found the homemade sodas to be flavorless and insipid.

Although Moby is co-owner of the restaurant with his ex-girlfriend Kelly Tisdale, he likens himself to a Victorian father who sees the baby only now and then. He writes the checks but Kelly does the day-to-day running of the shop. In providing such delicious fare in such a tastefully designed space, however teeny--Moby has done the community a whale of a service. Incidentally, Moby, (nee Richard Melvile Hall), is nicknamed after the whale in his distant ancestor, Herman Melvile's novel Moby Dick. He is a committed vegan; one could only wish that he had extended his veganism to the entire menu. Vegan dishes are marked with an asterisk.

TIEN GARDEN [ve] **$$**

Counter service

170 Allen Street
at E. Houston/ 1st Avenue

Chinese Homestyle
All cards
No alcohol
vegan@tiengarden.com

212-388-1364
Daily noon-10pm

Not so long ago, Tiengarden was a lonely outpost of veganism on the lower East Side. Now it may be seen as something of a neighborhood trendsetter. Within the past two years it has become surrounded by eco-conscious stores like Earth Matters and Bluestockings; tony vegan boutiques like MooShoes, and Organic Avenue; and fashionable vegetarian restaurants like Teany.

Based on the ancient theory of five elements--metal, water, earth, and fire--the food at Tiengarden is prepared in such a way as to maximize its chi, or life force. On the other hand, foods that are considered to be sapping of one's chi are scrupulously avoided. So in addition to being vegan, (because animal products are considered to be deleterious to one's chi); the dishes contain no garlic, or onions, which are also held to be harmful to one's chi. Nonetheless, the food is quite delectable without these flavor intensifiers.

We are partial to their Spicy-Fruity (spicy gluten nuggets with mango, tomato and red chili peppers in a piquant orange sauce) ,. We also ate with gusto their Burdock dumplings, but were disappointed with their Ginger Buckwheat noodles with Goji berries. The noodles were too soggy, and friable from being overcooked.

Recently, (May 2013), Tiengarden was remodeled, its menu, drastically revised. Instead of being a full-service restaurant with a waiter in attendance, it's now a self-service grab-and-go place. The room is now dominated by a photographic mural of a waterfall in China. Individual tables have given way to communal tables. [The bathroom, unfortunately, has been eliminated.] Beverages and prepared desserts are now set forth in a refrigerated display case. However, the food is as tasty as ever and is still based on the five-element theory.

WILD GINGER [v] $$ 👍

Full service
Pan-Asian
All cards
Beer, wine & sake
www. wildgingervegan.com

380 Broome Street
bet. Mott/ Mulberry Streets
212-966-1883/ 2669
daily 12pm-11pm

Three friends--Richard, (the architect and co-manager), Winnie (the accountant and manager), and her husband, Tim (the chef)--have pooled their assets, as it were, to create one of the most popular and successful vegetarian restaurants in town. Richard is responsible for the elegant yet cozy interior; Winnie, for the crisply efficient running of the place; and Tim for the tasty dishes. "Pan Asian" is how they describe their cuisine--Thai, Chinese, Malaysian and Indian--and for once the menu truly deserves this overused and often inaccurate appellation.

We practically shouted our adulation of the Scallion Pancakes with the Home-Made Mango Salsa, which tasted less like crepes than small pizzas topped with a piquant mango sauce. We adored the Samosa in Curry Sauce. Their newest appetizer, Tempeh in Satay Sauce is supernal. For the main course, our taste buds thrilled to the exotic flavor notes in Malaysian Curry Stew (Mild, Slow-Cooked Coconut Curry with Soy Protein, Broccoli, Carrots, Potatoes and Pumpkin). and Mango Soy Protein (Thin-Slice Medallions Sautéed in a Mellow Plum Sauce with Mango, Zucchini, Sweet-Sage Turnips, Peppers, and Onions).

Beverages--we tossed off the homemade Wild Ginger Beer, and Virgin Mojitoes with gusto. They were--at least to our teetotal, non-alcoholic sensibilities-- bewitching. For drinkers of more adult beverages, there is an array of beers, wine and sakes that are guaranteed to "bewitch, bother and bewilder." Vegans, however, should beware the Lassis (an Indian drink made with fruit juice and yogurt). Order soy-milk Lassis instead!

Chef Tim accrued his repertoire of Pan-Asian vegan dishes by working in a string of different veg. restaurants--such as Zen Palate, Tien Garden and assorted others--as a sous-chef. But by now, Tim has clearly outstripped his masters; so while one may recognize many of the menu dishes from having dined elsewhere, seldom have they been prepared to such palate-pleasing perfection.

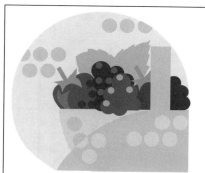

Congratulations:

The Vegan Guide to New York City

On Your 20th Anniversary!
Keep Up the Excellent Work!

...Compliments of a Friend

BELOW CANAL STREET
(Includes Chinatown, Tribeca, Financial District)

BUDDHA BODAI VEGETARIAN RESTAURANT [v] **$$**

Full service
Chinese (kosher)
All cards
No alcohol.

5 Mott Street
at Bowery
212-566-8388
daily 10:30am-10:30pm

See description under Queens

CRISP-3 [v] **$**
Counter service
Israeli-Indian falafel shack
All major cards
No alcohol
Eatatcrisp.com

111 Fulton Street
bet. William/ Dutch Streets
212-321-2200
daily 10am-10pm
Sa-Su 12pm-8pm

See description under Midtown West.

HOUSE OF VEGETARIAN [v] **$**

Full service
Chinese Homestyle
No cards
11pm
Beer & wine

68 Mott Street
bet. Canal/Bayard Streets
212-226-6572
daily 11am

This is one Chinatown restaurant where there aren't any fresh kills hanging in the window. "All We Are Served Vegetarian Dishes" reads the reassuring note on the extensive menu of more than 200 dishes, from Vegetarian Roast Duck (too much of a poultry flavor for our taste) to Braised Chicken with Lily Flowers (made from wheat gluten) or everybody's favorite, Iron Steak, made from yams and quite tasty. Our own personal favorite were mock Chicken with Mango and Black Mushrooms With Soysticks. Served in a narrow dining room with plastic tablecloths and no ambiance, but the food's good and there's plenty of it.

MAGIC MIX JUICERY [v] **$** 👍

Counter service
Organic juice bar cafe
All major cards
No alcohol
magicmixjuicery.com

102 Fulton Street
at William Street
646-454-0680
M-F 7:30am -8pm
Sa, Su 9am-s5pm

For many years, Jil Larsen, the owner of Magic Mix (she spells her first name with one "l") Juicery, toiled unhappily at a white shoe law firm; then suddenly she came down with melasmia-- a skin condition in which dark streaks appear on the skin's surface. This turned out to be the proverbial "blessing in disguise." Despite her doctor's remonstrations, she decided to treat the disorder holistically with juice fasting. Almost immediately, she began to see results; so she started studying nutrition formally, and earned a degree from the school of Integrative Nutrition. Eventually, she went vegetarian, quit her tedious job at the law firm and opened a spiffy new juice bar, purveying organic juice concoctions, smoothies, and main-course raw meals-- the Magic Mix Juicery. Its interior is modeled on the Apple stores with their luminous geometric white spaces.

We started with the Iron Man Kale Salad (Organic marinated kale, mixed with spinach, avocado, purple cabbage, shitake bacon, carrots, hemp seeds, Brazil nut parmesan, and house made spirulina dressing.) This made for a very satisfying and fortifying meal. We particularly liked the Shitake bacon bits that flecked the salad. And although it was well past the time for a matutinal meal, we bolted the most delicious breakfast dish that we've ever had for supper— Exotic Strawberry Banana Toast (House made strawberry banana bread topped with organic mixed fruit and vanilla maca coconut kreme). We accompanied them with two green juices— Green-Eyed Candy, and Detox Painkiller. Jil just turned 30, last August. To have founded New York City's incomparably best veg. juice bar café at such a tender age is a tribute to her entrepreneurial verve--to say nothing of her talent for improvising exquisite raw food juices, meals and snacks.

TERRI (Financial District) [ve] **$**

Counter service	100 Maiden Lane
Vegan gourmet fast food	bet. Pearl / Gold Streets
All major cards	212-742-7901
No alcohol	M-F 7am-10pm
www.Terrinyc.com	Sa Su 10am-9pm

See description and other location in Midtown West

VEGETARIAN DIM SUM HOUSE [ve] **$$**

Full service	24 Pell Street
Chinese	at Mott Street
No cards	212-577-7176
No alcohol	daily 11am-11pm

Vegetarian Dim Sum House serves most of the same dishes that its sister restaurant, House of Vegetarian, serves except that it offers them amid posher surroundings with a wider range of dim sum dishes. "Dim Sum" (literally "cooked snacks") are the snack-like dishes that are popular in Hong Kong, Taiwan and other parts of South China. The Cantonese like to put together several dim sum dishes for breakfast, lunch and tea; they even have a few dim sum dishes as appetizers before dinner. Because they may eat dim sum three or four times a day, these snacks have to be skillfully prepared to avoid boring the jaded palate. The dim sum that we had at the Dim Sum House were certainly unboring. We particularly liked the Spinach Dumpling, the Lotus Root Cake, and the Sticky Rice wrapped in Lotus Leaf. From the main course menu, we liked the mock roast duck and the mock chicken dishes made from tofu skin. Portions are generous and service is attentive.

Indicates we especially recommend this restaurant for the quality of the food

BROOKLYN

BLISS [v] $$

Full service
Natural
No cards
No alcohol

191 Bedford Avenue
bet. N6th / N7th Streets
718-599-2547
daily 8am-11pm

"Bliss was it in that dawn to be alive and eating brunch at Bliss, but to be vegetarian was very heaven!" is what Wordsworth might have written had he been a vegetarian and had he had the good fortune to dine at Bliss--one of New York's better vegetarian restaurants. He would surely have waxed poetic over the vegan BLT's that are made with Fakin' Bacon, the Veggie Burgers and the Seitan "Steak" Sandwiches. The salads are a tone poem and the desserts an ode to Bliss. With prices so much lower in Williamsburg than for comparable fare in Manhattan, it's worth hopping the L train and traveling East just one stop from Manhattan for so much more bliss for the buck.
    • Recent visits, in late 2013, yielded less bliss for the buck. It's façade is as unprepossessing as its food,, which now includes eggs and dairy products, but it's still worth a subway jaunt—to its sister establishment a few blocks away on Grand Street—Bliss Grand. *Vide infra.*

BLISS GRAND [ve] $$ 👍

Full service
Vegan cafe
All major cards
Beer & Wine
www.blissgrand.com

167 Grand Street
at Bedford Avenue
718-302-4726
Tu-F 7am-7pm
Sa, Sa 8am-7pm

Grand Bliss! An epithet not an expletive. Unaccountably, Bliss Grand has the same ownership as Bliss, but the contrast couldn't be starker, i.e. between Bliss and Grand Bliss. The food at Bliss Grand is worthy of the restaurant's name—Grand and Blissful! 'First of all, it's 100% vegan, whereas the food at Bliss is tainted by eggs and dairy products. The dishes at Bliss Grand are exotic and innovative; while those at Bliss are as lackluster as the peeling sign on its storefront façade. We loved their kale salad, and their Pulled Jackfruit Burger; Fact is, the latter was so toothsome and exotic that we nominated it for best vegan burger of 2014. We also deeply relished their jackfruit tostida. Everything we tried was superb, not to say blissful! Even the bless pie, which was so good that it should rather be called Grand Bliss Pie. The coffee too was fresh and flavorful, and blissfully grand.

BODY AND SOUL [ve] $

Food stand
International, organic
No cards
No alcohol

Farmers' Market
at Grand Army Plaza
212-982-5870
Sa 8am-4pm
Sa 8am-4pm

One of the best ways to keep body and soul together in the city is to have a light vegan meal at the vegan food stand in the Grand Army Plaza Farmers' market., which is called aptly enough Body and Soul. Started by the owners of Counter restaurant back in 1994, it draws throngs of hungry folk for breakfast, lunch, early light suppers, and snacks. And it's easy to see why. The out-size wraps and turnovers are scrumptious. Try the Saffron Potato wrap which teases the palate with plantain chunks hidden inside. Or try the Spinach Portabello Turnover, which is filled with tofu ricotta, and tastes a bit like a Spinach Lasagna. You might want to complement this with a dairy-free Blueberry Muffin, Or a Sweet Potato Muffin. Don't leave the stand without biting into a melt-in-your-mouth Chocolate Brownie, or a Wheat-Free Almond Cookie. Then repair to one of the benches in Prospect Park and have an *al fresco* meal.

CHAMPS [ve]] $

Counter service
Sandwich & salad cafe
Cash only
No alcohol
www.champsbakeryscom

176 Ainsle Street
at Leonard Street [Williamsbug]
718-599-2743
M-Sa 12pm-10pm
Su 12pm-6pm

The aptly named "Champs" is the undisputed champion among the vegan bakeries in NYC*, For complex pastries such as croissants, cinnamon swirls, and Danish pastries, they are simply unrivaled. While brunching there, we met one of the Champ bakers, a lady named Evan, who is a real craftsman of baked comestibles. At her suggestion, we tried the three-berry-filled Danish. We haven't had Danish since childhood, but this was the best Danish we've ever tasted, ever!

Next, we had chocolate cinnamon swirls. We also munched a chocolate chip cookie whose chips are impeccably vegan (from Tropical Source). As any self-respecting vegan toll house cookie should be, they were chewy and gooey and crunchy-but Champs' are a cut above the rest.. We chased all those sweet comestibles with Gimme Fair Trade Iced Coffee (which they soak rather than brew). We left the bakery feeling as if we were vegan fly-weight champs of the world.Recently, in the wake of their closing their sandwich shop, Boneshakers, Champs expanded its menu to include vegan savory dishes like Tofu Scramble and Hot Cubano.

*Except for Clementine Bakery, the new undisputed champ, but it's owner Michelle trained at Champs. *Vide infra*.

CLEMENTINE BAKERY [v]] $ 👍

299 Greene Street
Bet. Franklin/ Classon Avenues

Counter service
Bakery cafe
All major cards
No alcohol
www.clementinebakery.com

718-483-8788
Tu-F 9am-9pm
Sa 9am-9pm
Su 9am-6pm

We first learned of Clementine when we dined recently at Wild Ginger on Smith Street, where Richard Swanson, one of the owners, raved to us about the Clementine Brownie. Did we want to order one? Sure enough, it was the best brownie we'd ever tasted. Are all their baked goods like this? We wondered. Yes, and they make savories too. We couldn't get to Clementine fast enough. Next day, we ascertained for ourselves just how delicious the sweets and savories were. Amid the retro ambience that is redolent of the city's other vegan sweet shops-- Dun-Well Donuts, or Blythe Boyd's vegan ice-cream parlor-- we started with a Danish pastry. Surprisingly, it turned out to be a savory not a sweet. It was stuffed with tomatoes and sweet potatoes (with skins intact). Super-yummy! Then we tucked into their most popular sandwich—the Autumnal. It comprised barbecued tempeh, lettuce, tomatoes, sweet potatoes (with skins intact). Sensational! Next we shared the Tempeh Reuben (tempeh, apple, sauerkraut, Daiya mozzarella, Thousand Island dressing). Stupendous! We concluded the meal with a Cinnamon Bun (made of moist flaky dough, glazed with brown sugar, studded with pecans)--with which the repast reached a crescendo. What we particularly like about such sweets as the lemon-raspberry muffin, and strawberry-grapefruit cookie, etc. is that they're not over-sugared; they don't send one into insulin shock like those of a certain out-of-town vegan bakery, which shall be nameless in this review. Clementine opened on March 4th of last year, its owner Michelle's birthday—a day we should all celebrate as Clementine is easily the best vegan bakery in NYC, if not the cosmos!

DAO PALATE [v] $$

329 Flatbush Avenue
at Seventh Avenue

Full service
Pan Asian
All cards
Beer, wine & sake
www. Daopalate.com

718-638-1995/1998
N-Th 12pm -11:pm
F-Su 12pm-11:30pm
Su 12pm-10:30pm

If you have eaten at any of the wonderful Wild Ginger restaurants in the city [There are three altogether.]--you will have a sense of déjà vu when you dine at Dao Palate. The menu is almost identical to that of Wild Ginger. This duplication has come about because the owner of Tao Palate, Yuan-Yao Dong, is a distant relative of the co-owner of two other Wild Gingers. The story is a family saga that is far too convoluted to be deconstructed here. Suffice it to say that the cuisine, which Yuan-Yao describes as "Pan-Asian," [Malaysian, Indian, Korean, Japanese and Chinese], is several cuts above the rest.

On entering, we were struck by the three statues of the Buddha that smile beneficently on the non-violent feeding. The room is tastefully decorated with hammered brass sculptures on the exposed brick walls.

We started with crispy vegetable tofu skin wraps with tangy sauce, that were addictively tasty. Then we had the Mango Soy Protein with Vegetables in Plum Sauce, which was sumptuously exotic to the taste. This was accompanied by Pineapple Fried Rice, which we particularly prized because the pineapple, broccoli, and avocado chunks were flash-cooked so that they retained their true flavors. For dessert, we had their delectable Three-Berry Cheese Cake, in which the flavor of each berry seemed to be individuated.

We closed the meal with a mug of fair trade coffee, lightened with soy-milk, and sweetened with agave nectar. As we sipped this warm beverage, it struck us forcibly that the restaurant was aptly named: Tao (the ideal path) for the Palate.

• On a recent visit we found that the quality and service had fallen off. The dishes were rushed out, perfunctorily prepared; and the waitress removed our plates before we were done. They were more interested in turning over the table than providing good service. The check was also foisted on us before we had finished our desserts.

DUN-WELL DOUGHNUTS [ve] **$** 👍   222 Montrose Avenue

Counter service   at Bushwick Street
Vegan doughnut shop   347-294--0871
Cash only   Tu-F7am-7p
No alcohol   Sa, Sa 8am-7pm
www.dunwelldoughnuts.com

Only a city of NYC's immense population density could support so many single-item food purveyors such as New York Dosas, the Hummus Place, Pommes Frites, Moshe's Falafel, or Stogo's / Lula's vegan ice-cream parlors. Among the latest and best of these is Dim-Well Doughnuts in East Williamsburg, Brooklyn. [It's the 5th stop on the "L" Line.]

Founded by Dan Dunbar and Chris Hollowell --(who took the first and last syllables of their respective surnames to form Dun-Well)---Dun-Well has been open only a little more than a year, but it has already been crowned best doughnut emporium in the city by the New York Daily News. Which was quite a feat in light of the NYDN food reporter's self-admitted bias against veganism.

At Ithaca college, where Chris and Dan were vegan chums, they longed to open an ethical vegan business in New York City; but they were stymied by the lack of a BIG IDEA. Then suddenly, it hit them. While watching an episode of The Simpsons-(which has already given us the vegan cartoon goddess, Lisa Simpson,)--they were inspired by Homer Simpson's penchant for endlessly munching doughnuts to launch a vegan doughnut business.

Mentored by the owners of Lula's vegan ice-cream parlor, Blythe and Derek—Dan and Chris fitted out their store with a retro look and started baking the best vegan doughnuts on the planet. Peanut Butter and Jelly, Blueberry, Lemon Lavender and Chocolate Glaze are among their most popular flavors. Soon they will be offering savory doughnuts; so that one will actually be able to have a multi-course meal consisting exclusively of doughnuts! For the record, we like our Seitan Piccata well-done, and our doughnuts Dun-Well.

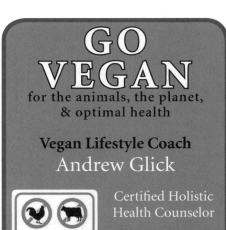

FOODSWINGS [ve] **$** 👍

Counter service
Fast food
Cash only
No alcohol

295 Grand Street
bet. Roebling/ Havemeyer
718-388-1919
Su-Th 11:30am-12am
F, Sa 11:30am-2am

Foodswings underwent a change of ownership--and a change of appearance--in early 2009.The former owner, Freedom Tripodi had put his unique eatery on the auction block. Happily, it was purchased by dedicated vegans with business acumen—Jeff and Hope--who are also owners of New York's (and possibly the world's) only vegan saloon--Lucky 13 (in Park Slope). Co-owner, Jeff Blanchard, is also a bassist, vocalist and founding member of the rock group, Eyes of the Sun.

Recently we swung by to see how the new Foodswings stacked up against the old. We're delighted to report that the animal rights spirits that pervaded the old Foodswings are still palpable. The walls are festooned with PETA posters; and brochures from nearby animal sanctuaries still abound.

Not incidentally, they still serve the best French fries in the cosmos! [Studies have shown that people go to the Golden Arches and other burger joints mainly for the French fries.] Their mock Chicken Cutlet sandwich on a Kaiser bun is still as tasty as it ever was. We also noted some improvements: They now make their own seitan from scratch; so that the flavor of their Homemade Chili Con Seitan is greatly enhanced by it. They make their Grilled Cheese Sandwich; their Mock Ham and Cheese Sandwich--along with many of their other sandwiches that contain mock cheese--with vegan Daiya Cheese. Made from cassava (tapioca), it's gooier and cheesier than any other ersatz cheese we've tasted.

Still the best-selling item on the menu, their Gyro-- (Seasoned mock beef with lettuce, tomato, red onion with vegan Tzatziki sauce.)—rules! Although we prefer their Sausage & Pepper Hero (Homemade vegan Italian sausage with peppers and onions on Italian bread.)

What's fast food without a soy-milkshake chaser? We chased ours with a Pistachio Shake (their Basic Shake with vegan pistachio ice-cream). They've increased the seating capacity of the room and have added a bathroom, the lack of which was one of the few drawbacks of the old Foodswings. Yes, dear reader, the new Foodswings is truly a swinging place to eat!

FOUR SEASONS RESTAURANT [ve} **$**

Counter service
Caribbean vegetarian
$4.00-10.00 [no cards}
No alcohol

2281 Church Avenue
at Bedford Avenue
718-693-7996
M-Th 9am-10pm
Fr-Sa 9am-12; Su 11am-7pm

This is not to be confused with the higher rent, higher cholesterol restaurant of the same name in Manhattan. This is the healthier vegetarian version. It's Fresh Assorted Curries, Vegetarian Lo Mein, Vegan Baked Goods and Fresh-Squeezed Juices will delight your palate and are guaranteed to ward off a thrombosis.

GOVINDA'S KITCHEN [v] $

Self service
Vaishnava Indian cuisine
No cards
No alcohol

305 Schermerhorn Street
bet. Nevins/ Bond Streets
718-885-6714
M-F 11:30am-3pm

In India, the Viashnava sect of Hinduism is known as the kitchen religion,--such is the prowess of its temple chefs. In the basement of this Hare Krishbna temple is a small cafeteria-style restaurant, where you may sample the cuisine of the American branch of this sect. It's not quite up to that of the Vaishnava temples of India, but it is very, very good, and reasonably priced with generous portions. We highly recommend the baked tofu, the *aloo gobi*, the quinoa salad, and the *gobi masla*. Unfortunately, not all dishes are vegan; so you should avoid the *palak paneer*, or anything with *paneer* in it.

JUICE PRESS, THE [ve] $$

Counter service
Organic Juices and raw food
All Cards
No alcohol
Thejuicepressonline.com

144 North 8th Stret
bet. Bedford/ Berry
212-777-0034
daily 8am-10pm

For description see East Village, and other locations passim.

LOVING HUT [ve] $

Full service
Pan Asian
All Cards
No alcohol
www.lovinghutnyc.com

76 Bushwick Avenue
at Power Street
718-388-7567
Su-Th 11am-11pm
F, Sa 11am-12am

This is the new Loving Hut that we've all been waiting for. It has much more elbow room (30 tables), and the same lip smacking cuisine as its sister restaurant in midtown Manhattan.. We relished the Sweet Vermicelli (Rice vermicelli noodles topped with seasoned stewed protein, pickled cucumbers, carrots, and crushed peanuts in a sweet and sour sauce). We also enjoyed the Spicy Cha Cha (Spicy seasoned yam-based sea protein, bell peppers and celery, served on romaine lettuce). The menu, however is entirely different; form that of the mid-Manhattan branch [but just as mouthwatering], so one may double one's pleasure by dinning at both locations

MAIMONIDE OF BROOKLYN [ve]] $

Full service
Vegetarian, kosher, gluten free
All Cards
Beer & wine
www.Mob-usa.com

525 Atlantic Avenue
bet. 4th/ 3rd Avenues
718-797-2555
Tu-F 9am-12am; Sa 11am-12am
Su 11am-5pm

When you sit down at one of the four large communal tables at Maoimonide, you are given a comic book manifesto, "The Awesome Genesis: Vol. I," that tells you the story of how the restaurant was founded by Cyril Aquizerate, a hip Paris hotelier and restaurateur, and how Maimonide got its name. It was named for Moses Maimonides the great Jewish physician-philosopher, who flourished in the 12th century CE. He was renowned for his *Guide for the Perplexed;* his commentary on the Mishna; and his treatises on diet and health.

We removed out eating utensils from a drawer in the table, and started with the Corn Soup with a side of curried Popcorn, and the Oyster Mushroom Chick-Pea Nuggets, which although baked, were still moist. However, we had to ask for a different dipping sauce for the nuggets, as the honey-mustard sauce that normally accompanies them was obviously not vegan. The MOB folks seem not to be cognizant that honey is not vegan; so ethical vegans beware. Many of the dishes, especially the desserts contain bee regurgitate.

Next we had the Moroccan flatbread pizza, which was more like an open-faced sandwich, allegedly in the shape of the arches of the Brooklyn Bridge. It was topped with roasted eggplant, pistachios and cilantro. My companion, Chris, had the Brave Heart flatbread pizza, which was topped with sun-dried tomatoes, kale, and mushrooms. Both went down very well.

We shared a fluffy quinoa salad with a lime dressing. For dessert, we had the lemon cheesecake, because it was the only dessert that our waiter could assure us was impeccably vegan. Like every other dish we tried, it was superb.

NILE VALLEY ECO-JUICE & SALAD BAR [ve} $

Counter service
Caribbean vegean
Cash only
No alcohol

138 Willoughby Street
bet. Albee Sq./ Prince Street
212-529-9262
Daily 11am-5pm

Like so many of the other storefront businesses in this pop-up market in downtown Brooklyn, the Nile Valley is housed in a recycled cargo container; but its vivid décor, and its exquisite food belie its humble origins. The "Nile Valley" is an allusion to Ethiopia, and the Rastafarian religious ethos that pervades the atmosphere in this eatery. We started with a mock tuna wrap that contained chopped walnuts, shredded carrots, red cabbage, cucumbers, and chunks of avocado. My companion downed a vegan hot dog and a kale smoothie. There were also salads galore,a raw pizza, and several pizzas made with the vegan Daiya "cheese" that made us look forward to a return visit.

PERELANDRA [v] $ 👍

Counter service
International
All Cards
No alcohol
www. perelandra natural.com

175 Remsen Street
bet. Court/ Clinton
718-855-6068
M-F 8:30-8:30
Sa 9:30-8:30:
Su 11-7

On their way to work, Brooklyn's pinstripe brigade pauses here just long enough to scarf down the Breakfast Sandwich, which is Perelandra's answer to the ghastly EggMaguffin (sic.). The Perelandra version consists of baked tofu, tempeh bacon, avocado, dill, and caramelized onion served on a Freshly Baked Spelt Muffin. Yummmy! Organic oatmeal with a different fresh fruit is served daily.

The pinstriped set returns for lunch, and it is not uncommon to see a long line of men and women in business suits standing politely in a line that insinuates itself through the store (Brooklyn's largest health food store). With courts and investment houses hard by, we are in Brooklyn's legal and business district. Eaten up with curiosity, we eavesdropped on the line-waters'c onversations: Sure enough, torts as well as tortes were being hotly discussed.

Every day Perelandra's menu changes, but the categories remain the same. For instance, every day they offer a Soup; a Sauce and Grain, A Casserole a Sandwich: a Wrap; an Entree and a Dessert.

For lunch we slurped their fresh Miso Soup; then savored the Japanese Wasabi Potato Salad and a Barbecue Un-Chicken Sandwich. We also sampled their Baked Vegetable Risotto. For the grand finale, we downed their inimitable Tofu Vegan Cheesecake. For the post prandial beverage, we sipped their Avocado Smoothie. Which contains Coconut Juice, Avocado, Agave Nectar, and Fresh Lime Juice. We specifically requested that they make it with Agave nectar as they ordinarily make it with honey. After the ethical sweetener were added, we tossed it off with gusto! Replete with delilcous vegan food and drink, we wobbled through the store's portal into a sun-splashed Brroklyn summer afteroon.

'sNICE II [v] $

Self service
Sandwiches, salads, baked goods
All cards
Beer & wine

315 5th Avenue
at 3rd Street
718-788-2121
daily 7:30am-10pm

See description under Greenwich Village

STRICTLY VEGETARIAN [ve] **$**

Counter service
Carribean vegetarian
$4.00-8.00 (no cards)
No alcohol

2268 Church Avenue
bet.Bedford/Flatbush Avenues
718-284-2543
daily noon-11:30pm

Just down the street from the late Veggie Castle with which it can stand comparison, this place serves such delicious Caribbean vegetarian dishes as Chick Pea Stew, Vegetable Chow Mein and Tofu Stew. The menu changes daily.

SUN IN BLOOM [ve] **$$**

Full service
Organic vegan gourmet
All cards
www. suninbloom.com

460 Bergen Street
bet. Flatbush/ Fifth Avenues
718-622-4303
dairly 8am-8pm
Brunch Sa-Su

Amy Follette used to run the Bikram Yoga School in Park Slope for 5 years. Where she also counseled her yoga students (and a few outside clients) on adopting a plant based diet, which is a prerequisite of classic yoga training. Though fulfilled in her work, she always had an urge to open a vegan restaurant. Then last January, Organic Heights went out of business, and she had an option to open a restaurant on the vacant site. So she sprang at the chance.

Bikram's loss is our gain, because the food that she prepares at Sun In Bloom may be described only with superlatives.

We started with Irresistible Granola Delight--a kefir with coconut milk base---to which she had added a vegan granola and chopped peaches. Divine!

Then we tucked into her Bloom Burger- a live burger made with sprouted, dehydrated sunflower seeds, and cabbage, layered with fresh tomatoes, crunchy, caramelized onions, and slathered with a live ranch dressing. It was much the best burger, we've ever tasted, raw or cooked.

Next we had her Reuben Special which features "corned" tempeh with a mountain of live sauerkraut, served with a kitchen-fresh Russian dressing with a dash of dulse. Sublime!

While we downed our food, we sipped two terrific smoothies--an Acai Punch, which consisted of acia, raw apple cider vinegar, soymilk, frozen bananas and strawberries that really packed a punch. We also quaffed her Ambrosia Smoothie (young coconut, raw cacao, raw goji berries, raw almond butter, coconut kefir yogurt, banana, and strawberries.) Truly ambrosial!

For dessert we had a live Peach Cheesecake composed of a cashew cheese, and fresh peaches.

Amy is on a mission to get people to eat food that is directly created from photosynthesis--Sun Food ,as it were--rather than being filtered through the bodies of animals. Judging from the high quality of her food, the hygienic freshness of her sun-splashed restaurant, she is poised for success.

• On a recent visit to SIB, a little more than a year after they opened,, we found that they had installed a restroom, and expanded their brunch menu, which is available on weekends from10am-5pm. We sampled one of their brunch specials, which has proved so popular that it is now featured on their regular menu. This was their gluten free pancake stack. Topped with caramelized bananas, seasonal fruit and a splash of maple syrup, it went down very well.

TINY EMPIRE [ve] $$

Counter service
Organic rawjuice bar
All cards
info@tinyempirenyc.com

142 North 6th Street
bet. Bedford/ Berry Streets
718-599-5575
daily 8am-8pm

We asked Anthony, the owner of Tiny Empire, how it got its name. He answered that you can build an empire of health from one bottle of cold-pressed organic juice, such as their best-selling #7, a blend of kale, green apple, celery, ginger, and lemon. It was made with the Good Nature cold press juicer, which has superseded the Norwalk Juicer in extracting the phytonutrients from fruits and vegetables. You can also build your tiny empire from the appetizing range of organic dehydrated snacks as well as a tasty array of organic salads and desserts that are on offer.

V-SPOT CAFE, THE [ve] $$ 👍

Full service
Latin cuisine
All cards
Beer, wine, & spirits
thevspotcafe.com

156 Fifth Avenue
bet. Douglass/ Degraw Streets
718-928-8778
T-Th 12pm -10:pm
F-Sa 11am-10pm
Su 11am-9pm

Verily an erogenous zone for the vegan palate is the Park Slope eatery called the "V-Spot" that is also Kosher certified via IKC Kosher. Here the dishes are in the uncensored words of a lady friend, who dines there often, "Sooooo gooood!" We certainly wanted to have what she was having; so we ventured over to V-Spot to see what all the fuss and bother was about. There in an intimate room, with the artwork of local New York artists adorning exposed brick walls, we savored the V-Spot experience.

Serious vegans, will be impressed by the V-Spot's dedication to ethical standards. Clearly the V in this V-Spot is not for Vendetta, but for Victory!

Alex, one of the co-owners, who often doubles as a waiter, took our order. A part-time stand up comedian, Alex hosts a monthly comedy night every first Thursday of the month at 10pm right in the establishment. He's been on national TV, but that didn't mean he was too busy to ensure we had lemon slices for our water. His brother Danny chatted with us about their famous homemade salsa recipe.

Most of the dishes on the menu are derived from family recipes--such as the appetizer Empanadas--that the brothers inherited from their Colombian paternal grandmother. Even the seemingly prosaic "Steak" with Sweet Plantains, Rice & Beans (Bandeja Paisa)--is reminiscent of the authentic *comida* to be had in the village cantinas of South America. Its authenticity--albeit veganized,--is why it, and so many of the other dishes with a Latin flair, are so utterly transporting. Danny also encouraged us to try selections from the fresh juice bar, and let us know about raw and gluten-free options.

The Latin flair extends to Italian specialties such as Whole-wheat Lasagna, "Chicken" Parmigiana, Quinoa Pasta Marinara, but the Veggie Tacos danced fandangos on our tongue. Piquant also were the side orders of Spinach with Garlic and Olive Oil or Curried Kale with Chickpeas. Other dishes we found particularly flavorful were an appetizer Raw Nori Rolls (A ginger almond pate surrounds a center of spinach, avocado and carrots) and an entree: Quinoa with Curried Kale. Desserts are the dependably scrumptious vegan treats like cupcakes or gluten-free brownies, as well as vegan ice-cream.

Can't make it out to Brooklyn? Well, the V-Spot is also successfully retailing popular food items in packages at locations throughout New York City. These items include their Organic Quinoa with Curried Chick Peas and Kale, Colombian Empanadas, Black Bean Empanadas and Sesame Tofu with Quinoa. These V Spot creations are also available through the online grocer, Fresh Direct at http://www.Freshdirect.com.

VEGETARIAN GINGER   [v] $$ 👍

	128 Montague Street (2nd Fl)
Full service	Corner Montague/ Henry Streets
Chinese	718-246-1288
All cards	M-Th 11:30am-10:30pm
No alcohol	Fr, Sa 11:30am,-11:00pm
www.vegetarianginger.com	Su: 12:00--10:00pm

It's great to see a new vegan Chinese restaurant on the site of the old Greens [a quondam vegan Chinese restaurant at the same location.], however, one wishes they weren't so derivative--in their title and in the quality of their food. There are already two Wild Gingers in Brooklyn and one Vegetarian Palate. So having one more Chinese vegan restaurant with ginger in the title merely adds to he confusion. Couldn't they have been a bit more inventive and called themselves something else? Jade Pumpkin? Red Persimmon? The Pink Fig? The Golden Peach? The food is flavorful here, and we particularly enjoyed the Smoked Teriyaki Seitan, The Malaysian Curry Stew, and the Jade Mushrooms, but the dishes, like the name of the restaurant itself, are lacking in originality

VEGETARIAN PALATE [v] $$ 👍

Full service
Chinese
All cards
No alcohol
www.vegetarianpalate.com

603 Washingron Avenue
Bet Dean / Pacific Streets
718-623-8808/9
M-Th 11:30am-10:30pm
Fr, Sa 11:30am,-11:30pm
Su 12:00--11:00pm

Vegetarian Palate probably has the most extensive menu of any vegetarian restaurant in the city. Which reminds us of the famous adage that you should never fall in love with someone who has more problems that you, or play cards with someone named "Doc," or eat in a restaurant named "Mom's,"--or in one that has a superabundance of items on the menu. Like most Chinese vegan restaurants Vegetarian Palate abounds in mock meats--as witness their vegetarian seafood dish, Ocean Harvest, which features a collection of vegetarian shrimp, scallops, and squid served with broccoli, snow peas, and baby corn. But the ultimate mock meat tour de force is their Paella Valencia , which is composed of sundry mock seafoods such as shrimp, scallops, crab, mock chicken, mock eel, tofu, shitake mushrooms with mixed vegetables. The service is crisply efficient, the decor, garish. Other diners have complained of excessive starch and oil in the dishes, but one may request of the waiter that these additives be omitted. We had the Soy Chicken with Spinach in Curry Sauce, and the Soy Lemon Chicken and our palates were beguiled by them. For dessert we indulged ourselves in a Banana Split, made with three scoops of non-dairy ice-cream covered with sprinkles and chocolate syrup--all of which soothed our vegetarian palate.

•As of earlier this year, Vegetarian Palate moved from Flatbush Avenue to its present location on Washington Avenue. Apparently, it must have been a smart move as the mock Mango Chicken seemed to taste better, and the place was packed!

WILD GINGER II [v] $$ 👍

Full service
Pan-Asian

212 Bedford Avenue
at North 5th Street
718-218-8828

WILD GINGER III [v] $$ 👍

Full service
Pan-Asian
All cards
Beer, wine & sake
www.wildgingervegan.com

112 Smith Street
bet. Pacific/ Dean Sreets
718-858-3880
Mon-Thu 11:30am-11pm Fri- &
F, Sat 11:30am-11:30pm
Sun 12pm-11pm

For description, see under Soho.

QUEENS

ANNAM BRAHMA [v] $

Full service
Indian vegetarian
$4.00-12.00 (all cards)
No alcohol

84-43 164th Street
at Hillside Avenue
718-523-2600
M-Tu,Th-Sa 11am-10pm
W 11am-4pm; Su 12-10pm

This year marks the 43rd anniversary of Annam Brahma, [They opened in 1971.],, making it one of the most venerable vegetarian restaurants in the city. It was started and is currently operated by followers of the spiritual leader Sri Chimnoy, who encourages his pupils to observe a vegetarian diet, to meditate and to give something back to the community. (Pictures of Chimnoy running marathons and striking poses festoon the walls). His pupils founded this restaurant to contribute to the common weal; and the high quality of the food bespeaks their dedication to higher principles. Particularly recommended are the delicious Chapati Roll-Ups that are stuffed with either an American Veggie Burger filling or an Indian Curry filling, and the Veggie Kebabs made with soy meat.

DOSA DELIGHT [v] $

Full Service
South Indian Vegetarian
All cards
No alcohol
www.dosa-delight.com

35-66 73rd Street
at 37th Avenue (Flushing)
718-397-1000
daily 11:30am-10pm

We ordered Pondicherry Dosas which come topped with a layer of hot chutney and a spicy mixture inside. They went down very smoothly as did the Vegetable Uthappams topped with onions and carrots, but there was a greasy aftertaste to the food that made it somewhat less delightful than we would have liked.

DOSA HUTT [v] $

Counter service
South Indian Vegetarian
No cards
No alcohol

45-63 Bowne Street
(Flushing)
718-961-5897
daily 10am-9pm

This is India's answer to the Pizza Hut. Dosas, which are enormous crepes filled with spicy potato mixtures, do bear a resemblance to pizza, but I'll take a dosa over a pizza any time. The dosas here are tip-top, We especially relished the Masala Dosa. As with Dossa Diner, they're bigger and cheaper here than in the Big Dosa!

HAPPY BUDDHA [ve] $

Full service
Chinese
All major cards
No alcohol
www.happybuddha.com

135-37 37th Avenue
(Flushing)
718-358-0079
daily 11am-10pm

There are a myriad of tasty dishes on the menu that would make the Buddha and any other vegan very happy indeed. The vegetarian mock duck was a personal favorite.

MAHARAJAH QUALITY [v] $
SWEETS & SNACKS

Full service
International vegetarian
All Cards
No alcohol

73-10 37th Avenue
bet. 73rd/ 74th Streets
718-505-2680
daily 10am-10pm

As with Shamiana, this is Indian cuisine at its most caseous. The sweets and the dishes in the back are awash in milk, yogurt, cream, ghee, butter and cheese. You can pick your way through the menu to find vegan dishes, but is it really worth it? Unlike Rojbhog Foods, and Raja Sweets, which are right across the street, the staff here are decidedly unfriendly to vegans.

NEW BUDDHA BODAI [v] $

Full service
Chinese (kosher)
All cards
No alcohol.

59-8 Main Street
at Cherry Avenue
718-909-1188
daily 11am-11pm

There is a wide array of dishes to choose from--Veg. Snail to Sweet and Sour Fish. Indeed, the range of ersatz is so exhaustive that it put us in mind of those Taoist temple kitchens in which chefs flaunt their ingenuity by creating ever more elaborate mock meat dishes. But we did not enjoy our dining experience here; mainly because the manager was brusque and discourteous and refused to entertain any questions as to which dishes were vegan and which were not.

ONENESS FOUNTAIN HEART [v] $$ 👍

	157-19 72md Avenue
Full service	(Flushing)
International vegetarian	718-591-3663
All cards)	daily 11:30-9pm
No alcohol	W 11:00-9:00

Yet another restaurant that is operated by disciples of Sri Chimnoy. In addition to the -blue facades that all the restaurants share, they also have in common an uncommon devotion to high culinary standards and service. The dishes to try here are the Duck Surprise, which is made with vegetarian mock duck, and the Vegetarian Meatloaf. My personal favorite was Thai Heaven, which consists of spicy tofu skin in a delicate coconut sauce. It's worth taking a cab from Manhattan for this one.

PANORAMA CAFE [v] $

	86-14 Parsons Boulevard
Counter service	(Jamaica)
International vegetarian	718-526-0723
No cards	M-F 7am-9pm
No alcohol	Sa-Su 9am-8pm
www.Panoramacafe.org	

This place may be suitable for the most lacto of lacto vegetarians, but it is far too caseous to be recommended for vegans. Unfortunately the dishes are overloaded with dairy and eggs (chick embryos.) While it is true that they offer Daiya cheese as a substitute, it is rather tedious to have to make substitutions for every dish. Although this is another of the Sri Chimnoy restaurants, and we would love to praise it, we could not find one vegan dish on the menu. We cannot give a favorable review to a restaurant that doesn't keep eggs and cheese to a minimum. This place is replete with them.

QUEENS KICKSHAW, THE [v] $

	40-17 Broadway
Full service	(Astoria)
International vegetarian	718-777-0913
All major cards	M-F 7:30am-1am
Beer & wine	Sa Su 9am-1am
www. Thequeenskickshaw.com	

The food here is well-crafted, and fleshless, and the owners are extremely nice, but The Queens Kickshaw is strictly for lacto-ovo vegetarians. Nearly all the dishes are caseous and ovular, and the few that aren't are commingled with egg and dairy molecules.

RAJBHOG FOODS [v] $

Counter service
Kosher Jaonf foods
All major cards
No alcohol
www. Rajbhog.com

72-27 37th Avenue
at 73rd Street (Jackson Heights)
718-458-8513

10am-10pm daily.

The menu changes daily. The owner Nrav Shah told us that they had been doing business in this very spot for 40 years. The neighborhood has changed since his family first opened the shop. Jackson Heights is no longer an exclusively Indian enclave. Vegan yuppies have infiltrated the area asking for vegan versions of traditional Indian dishes that may have contained milk, or ghee. Consequently, Nirav stands ready to make vegan versions of any dish that is on offer.

RAJA SWEETS & FAST FOOD[v] $

Counter service
Indian homestyle cuisine
All major cards
No alcohol
www. Raja.com

72-31 37th Avenue
at 73rd Street (Jackson Heights)
718-424-1850
10am-10pm daily.

Like Rajbhog foods with which is is cheek by jowl on 37th Avenue, the chefs here stand ready to serve vegan dishes, and are quite sensitive to the demands of vegan clients. Menus change daily.

SMILE OF THE BEYOND [v] $$

Counter service
International vegetarian
No cards
No alcohol

86-14 Parsons Boulevard
(Jamaica)
718-739-7453
M-F 7am-4pm
Sa 7am-3pm

Not all restaurants in Queens are run by followers of Sri Chimnoy, it only seems that way. This astoundingly inexpensive luncheonette serves delicious veggie burgers, and generous salads that would cost the earth in a Manhattan eatery. All three Chimnoy places are worth the trek from Manhattan. At this place, so economical are the prices that the train fare will probably end up costing more than the meal!

TEMPLE CANTEEN [v] $

Counter service
Hindu temple cuisine
All major cards
No alcohol

143 Holly Avenue-
at Bowne Street
718-460-8493
8:30am-9pm daily

Ganesh, the multiple-armed, elephant-headed son of Shiva is the presiding deity at the Hindu Temple Society in Flushing, Queens. Within the Temple Society and community center, are spacious halls that are used for weddings, and an auditorium where Indian musicians and dancers perform. In the basement of this temple complex is a wonderful restaurant where you may sample authentic Hindu temple cuisine.

The big draw here are the dosas and samosas that are among the tastiest in the Big Dosa. The big drawback is that they are cooked in *ghee* (clarified butter), which Hindus hold to be a sacred food. Therefore, it is imperative that as an ethical vegan, you tell the counterman to instruct the chef to prepare your food with corn oil, rather than ghee, (which they were more than willing to do for us.)

We highly recommend the plain Pondicherry Dosa. Made from lentil-rice flour that is folded into a large, flat triangle that easily exceeds the size of your plate, it is filled with spiced potato mash. My companion savored the Mysore Dosa, which is filled with spiced cauliflower mash mingled with sautéed onions.

The trick to eating a dosa with aplomb is to tear off a small chunk, (Make sure it contains some of the filling.), dip it into the coconut chutney, which accompanies each dosa, and eat with gusto!

VEGGIE CASTLE [ve] **$**

132-091 Liberty Avenue
near Van Wyck Expwy
718-641-8342
daily 10am-10pm

Counter service
Caribbean
All cards
No alcohol

Last year Veggie Castle moved to Queens from its original location in Brooklyn, where it had struck a decided blow for veganism and animal rights by turning a White Castle fast food restaurant into a vegan Rasta restaurant. When Veggie Castle first opened, it was as though the farm animals had revolted and taken over the farm! The hostages had overpowered their captors!

Some enterprising vegetarian business folks had actually taken over a former burger joint and turned it into a vegetarian restaurant that serves the Veggie Castle Burger along with an array of delicious dishes that you won't find in your typical fast food place--such as Curried Soy Chicken, BBQ Soy Chunks With Pineapple, and ersatz Shepherd's Pie. We had a Spicy Black Bean Burger that was much the best veggie burger we'd ever tasted. We followed this with an order of Turmeric Bean Curd Duck that really showed off to advantage the culinary talent of Veggie Castle's Rasta *chefs de cuisine*. Instead of soda pop and shakes, Veggie Castle's juice bar serves a range of fresh fruit/vegetable juices and smoothies. Veggie Castle is giving fast food such a good name that, in the future, all burger joints may be dishing up Wheat Grass Juice and Veggie Burgers. It's cause for hope.

THE BRONX

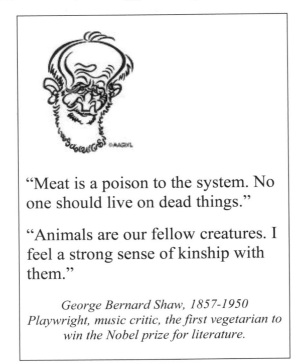

VEGAN'S DELIGHT [v] $$ 👍

Counter service
Organic Caribbean
All Cards
No alcohol

3565 Boston Road
at Tiemann Avenue
718-653-4140
M-Sa 8am-6:30pm

Like Healthy Pleasure and Imhoteps, in Queens and Brooklyn, respectively, Vegan's Delight is a combination health-food store and restaurant. Is it worth the trip from Manhattan to eat here? That depends: If you're a connoisseur of Ital food as we are, then the trip is certainly warranted. However, there are places in Manhattan and Brooklyn that do the Ital thing just as well if not better. For instance: The Uptown Juice Bar and Veggie Castle--to list but two. We savored the Curried Bean Curd, the Ital Stew, and the Eggplant Melange, and commend it to you.

"Meat is a poison to the system. No one should live on dead things."

"Animals are our fellow creatures. I feel a strong sense of kinship with them."

George Bernard Shaw, 1857-1950
Playwright, music critic, the first vegetarian to
win the Nobel prize for literature.

NEW PALTZ

KARMA ROAD [ve] **$** 👍

Full service
Global Organic cafe
All cards
No alcohol
www.karmaroad.net

11 Main Street
(Next to the bicycle depot)
845-255-1099
M-Sa 8am-8pm
Su 8am-6pm

There is an adage which has it that the road to good karma is paved with delicious vegan dishes. In fact, in all candor, we coined this adage after driving up from New York City and dining at Karma Road in New Paltz, NY, one of two vegan restaurants in Ulster County (The other is the great Garden Cafe in Woodstock. Both stand comparison with the very best vegan restaurants in NYC.)

Specifically after eating their delicious Karma Reuben Sandwich--(baked tempeh, sauerkraut, Russian dressing, and lettuce)--did we feel that our karma had been ameliorated. Even more so after we had their Karma Combo Salad (A festival of romaine lettuce, kale, celery, carrot, tomato, tossed in a topped with tahini dressing). We then tossed it off with a delicious Young Chocolate Coconut Shake (young Thai coconut meat, coconut water, agave and Dutch chocolate). For dessert we had their Ohmygod! chocolate cake. This one was one more scintillating dish for the road, the road to good karma!

Karma Road
Delicious Healthy Food For Everyone!

- ❤ Sandwiches, Soups, Salads, Deli

- ❤ Breakfast Burritos, Hot Cereal

- ❤ Wheat/Dairy-Free Aplenty

- ❤ Organic/Vegetarian

- ❤ Great Coffee

- ❤ Baked Goods

- ❤ Wi-Fi

Open 7 Days
Mon-Sat 8am-8pm, Sun 8am-6pm

11 Main St. New Paltz, NY. karmaroad.net

"The discovery of a new vegan restaurant dish does more for the well-being of the human race than the discovery of a new star."

...Jean Brillat Savarin (1756-1825)
[revised with apologies]

WOODSTOCK

GARDEN CAFE [v] **$$** 👍

6 Old Forge Road
(on the Village Green)
845-679-3600
W-M 11:30am-9pm

Full service
Gourmet global Organic
All cards
Organic wines & beers

One of our favorite New York escapes is to spend the weekend in Woodstock. It is still redolent of the arts colony that it used to be in the early part of the last century, and of the hippie era of the sixties. Now we can augment the pleasure of our weekend getaways by dining at the Garden Café. It was opened seven years ago by chef Pam Brown, Overflowing with energy and enthusiasm, she is wholly dedicated to cooking to the highest standard.

In addition to her regular lunch and dinner menus, daily specials include a Garden Bowl, consisting of greens, whole grains, vegetables, beans, tofu, tempeh, or seitan. We started with an Millet Squares with caramelized onions, Baked Tofu with Rosemary Roasted Pepper Gave with Sauteed Kale.

Then we tucked into an international array of dishes that included Indian Vegetable and Chickpea Enchiladas, served with a Bombay Sauce, and a Curried Apple-Coconut Salad on the side. *Sensationel!* We tossed this off with multiple toasts of organic vegan wine and beer. We also had the Southwest Black Bean and Roasted Sweet Potato Burger with Guacamole Salsa and a wedge of Vegan Cheddar. *Magnifique!* After downing these, our faces beamed with satisfaction.

We had to bolt in order to be on time for a concert at the Maverick; so we skipped the Strawberry Shortcake with vegan ice-cream. But we will be returning tomorrow night, [after we visit the Woodstock Farm Animal Sanctuary, and the Catskill Animal Sanctuary], to sit in reposeful ease under the poplar trees and gaze at the town square "thinking green thoughts in a green shade."

Garden Cafe

Eclectic cozy
vegetarian cafe
serving
mostly organic,
fresh,
local whole foods.

6 Old Forge Road
Woodstock, NY
(845) 679-3600

11:30AM– 9PM
Closed Tuesdays

ON THE GREEN

The Bronx

Harlem

125th Street

110th Street

[15]
Upper
West
Side

[9] [8]

Central Park

[8]

W 59th Street

E 59th Street

[3] [14]
Upper
East
Side [15]

East
River

Hudson
River

[22]
Midtown
[8] West

5th Avenue

Midtown
East

[4]
[1] [22]

[2]

[5]
[8] [8]
Chelsea
[6]

[13]

Gramercy Park

[22]

W 14th Street

E 14th Street

[6]

[9] [19]

Greenwich
Village

Broadway

[16]
East Village

[17] [10]
[8]

[20] [12]

Houston Street

Soho

Williamsburg
Bridge

[7] [5]

Canal Street

Tribeca

[21]

Chinatown

Brooklyn Bridge

Financial District

Brooklyn

Queens

[11]

FAVORITE RESTAURANTS

1. Franchia
2. Hangawi
3. Candle79
4. Kajitsu
5. Loving Hut
6. Beyond Sushi
7. Foodswings
8. Blossom/B. Du Jour
9. Peacefood Cafe
10. New York Dosas
11. The V-Spot
12. Caravan of Dreams
13. Terri
14. V-Note
15. Candle Cafe
16. Quintessence
17. Red Bamboo
18. Veggie Castle II
19. Jivamuktea Cafe
20. Lan Cafe
21. Vegetarian Dim Sum House
22. Zen Palate

TOP TEN JUICE BARS

Y

Although they don't yet outnumber the alcohol bars, or the coffee bars, juice bars are starting to crop up all over town. Unhappily, many of them--like Gray's Papaya--serve meat along with their smoothies and juices. [Recently, we had to drop Juice Generation for serving chicken sandwiches,, and Liquitira for serving tuna fish sandwiches.] So we picked places that serve only vegan dishes to go with their drinks. Not so long ago, New Yorkers used to start the day with a shot of bourbon or a mug of java; now, as like as not, they'll get their hearts started with a shot of "green plasma"--wheat grass juice, brimming with enzymes, anti-oxidants, chlorophyll, and phytonutrients.

MAGIC MIX JUICERY [v]

Counter service
Organic juice bar cafe

102 Fulton Street
at William Street

And although it was well past the time for a matutinal meal, we bolted the most delicious breakfast dish that we've ever had for supper—Exotic Strawberry Banana Toast (House made strawberry banana bread topped with organic mixed fruit and vanilla maca coconut kreme). We accompanied them with two green juices—Green-Eyed Candy, and Detox Painkiller..

THE JUICE PRESS [ve]   at 14 locations:

JP 1
70 East 1st Street
bet. 1st / 2nd Avenues

Consult neighborhood listings for all other locations

The Juice Press uses a Norwalk hydraulic press. (Up to five times more of the enzymes, minerals and vitamins are expressed in the juices by this method than by any other.) For a bracing sandwich, try JP' Schmear homemade vegan rosemary cream cheese and marinated cucumbers on a toasted sprouted grain bagel. . For a Smoothie, try the Rain Forest a refreshing blend of lemon, mint, coconut water, banana, and other tropical ingredients They're a ticket to esophageal paradise.

PEACEFOOD CAFÉ   at 2 locations

480 Amsterdam Avenu
at 82nd treet

PFC 2
41 East 11th Street
@ University Place

Although Peacefood Cafe is primarily a restaurant; the quality of the juices and smoothies surpasses that of most juice bars. Eric and his partner Peter select only the finest, most healthful ingredients for their delicious concoctions. We highly recommend their Passion Fruit Smoothie,, the Acai Berry Smoothie , as well as the ingenious juice blends such as the pineapple juice, beet, and lime concoction that we favor.

ORGANIC AVENUE [ve]   at 10 locations

OA 1
116 Suffolk Street
bet. Delancey/ Rivington Streets
212-358-0500
M-F 8am-8pm
Sa,Su 8am-10pm

We quaffed a Blueberry Smoothie and followed it with a Portobello Sandwich. For dessert, we ate their Coco-Lime Pie. All were surpassingly yummy. Unusually, after such a heavy meal, we felt strangely lifted and energized.

GREENER PASTURES [ve]

Union Square Greenmarket
16th St. / Union Square West
M,W, F, Sa 8am-7pm

On Mondays, Wednesdays, Fridays and Saturdays of every week, Stewart, the proprietor, serves up wheat grass juice and effervescent good humor to the patrons who mob his stand. They swear he has the sweetest grass in the city. A one ounce shot is $3.00 a double shot is $5.00. ;Recently; Stewart enlarged his repertoire of hices. He now offers a green juice combination, which consists of pea sprouts , sunflower spouts, carrots, apples, and ginger. The spouts are grown by Stewart at his indoor farm in Brooklyn; but the carrots, apples, and ginger are supplied by other farmers in the market; so their freshness and quality are guaranteed. This drink, served in capacious containers. The small is $5; the large is $7/. Stewart also sells flats of Wheat Grass as well as succulent salad greens.

UPTOWN VEG JUICE BAR [ve]

14 East 125th Street
daily 8am-10pm

They offer a wide array of juices and juice combinations that are designed to cure everything from asthma to impotence. The fruit smoothes are delicious, and the Caribbean style vegan food is first rate.

FOOD SHOPPING

I't's possible to eat cheaply in New York. It's also possible to spend your life savings on a single meal (though much easier for meat-eaters than for vegans!). This applies to restaurants as well as to shops, which range from the most luxurious importers to inexpensive, dependable local farm products. Below are some notable places that won't break your budget; for obvious reasons, this is not a comprehensive list. Individual addresses are listed on the following page.

SUPERMARKETS

these, and it The largest stores carry health food items, soy milk, and the like, but their prices are not usually any lower than large health food shops for these goods. The New York chains, listed in roughly ascending order of price (quality is quite similar):
Associated, Sloan's, Gristede's, Met Food, D'Agostino, Food Emporium, WholeFoods.

PRODUCE

There are greenmarkets, also called farmer's markets, on certain days in public squares, where producers drive truckloads of fresh and often organic fruits and vegetables into the city from their farms in upstate New York, Pennsylvania, and New Jersey. The prices and quality can't be beat, and there's a festive atmosphere to these events. Of course, you'll find only what's in season, so there are slim pickings during the cold winter months. Union Square is the largest of boasts a vegan bakery stall called Body & Soul with great treats both sweet and savory.

The next choice for organic produce is shopping at a large health food store like Wholesome Market, Integral Yoga or Commodities. Prices are a bit higher, but the quality is excellent.

For non-organic produce, the Asian shops along Canal Street in Chinatown and on First Avenue around 7th Street in the East Village have the lowest prices. Otherwise, supermarkets and the 24-hour groceries that line many New York streets are fairly reliable.

BULK GOODS, SPICES, ETC.

The larger health food shops all have a section where you can buy grains, beans, nuts, dried fruit, flour and snacks in bulk, most of it organic. For non-organic bulk goods and wonderful spices at low prices, try the Indian shops around Lexington and 28th Street or First Avenue and 6th Street.

FAVORITE SHOPS

HARLEM

FAIRWAY FRUITS & VEGETABLES
Huge produce and natural food store.

2328 Twelfth Avenue
at West 132nd Street

7 GRAINS HEALTH FOODS
Health food shop.

2259 Seventh Avenue
at 133rd Street

UPPER WEST SIDE

GARY NULL'S UPTOWN WHOLEFOODS

2307 Broadway
at West 89th Street

Health food grocery with bustling juice bar and kosher vegetarian salad bar.

HEALTH NUTS
Health food shop with juice bar.

2611 Broadway
at West 99th Street

WHOLEFOODS MARKET
Organic supermarket.

10 Columbus Circle
at 60th Street

UPPER EAST SIDE

HEALTH NUTS
Health food shop with juice bar.

1208 Second Avenue
bet. 63rd/64th Streets

MATTER OF HEALTH
health food shop with juice bar.

1478 First Avenue
at 77th Street

NATURAL FRONTIER
Organic grocery with emphasis on vegetarian and vegan.

1424 Third Avenue
at 81st Street

Books by Rynn Berry

FAMOUS VEGETARIANS
and their favorite recipes

Lives and Lore from Buddha to the Beatles

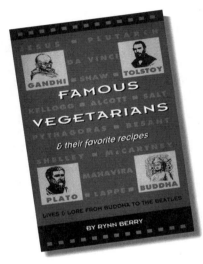

"Berry writes beautifully, with a genuine gustatory relish for words and savory asides. The recipes are delightful...many researched and translated for the first time." — *The Boston Book Review*

"Scholarship at the end of a fork — and for writing it Berry deserves an 'A'." — *Vegetarian Times*

"Entertaining and educational..." — *Vegetarian Voice*

"Impeccably researched and written." — *The Animals' Agenda*

"The 70 recipes are not only fascinating, but have been kitchen-tested by the author for savoriness..." — *Yoga Journal*

292 pages   **$15.95** *paperback*

Copy this form to order books. Other books by Rynn Berry on reverse side.

✂ ---

PYTHAGOREAN PUBLISHERS / P.O. Box 8174 / New York, NY 10116

——— copies *Famous Vegetarians & Their Favorite Recipes* @ $15.95	$ ———
——— copies *The New Vegetarians* @ $10.95	$ ———
——— copies *Food for the Gods* @ $19.95	$ ———

Add postage: $3.00 for one book, $1.00 for each additional book $ ———

TOTAL ENCLOSED $ ———

NAME _____

ADDRESS _____

CITY _____ STATE/ZIP _____ PHONE _____

ORGANIC MARKET
Health food shop.

229 Seventh Avenue
bet. 23rd/24th Streets

SIVANANDA YOGA VEDANTA CENTER
Exercise, breathing, relaxation, diet, and mediation

243 West 24th Street
bet. 7th/8th Avenues

WESTERLY NATURAL MARKET
Well stocked organic grocery.

911 Eighth Avenue
at 54th Street

WHOLEFOODS MARKET
Organic supermarket.

250 Seventh Avenue
at 24th Street

MIDTOWN EAST

BODY & SOUL
All-vegan baked goods stand.M F year-round.

Union Square Greenmarket
bet. 17th St / Union Sq.West

FANTASY FRUIT FARM
Blueberries, strawberries, raspberries, seedless grapes
Saturdays, June-Nov.

Union Square Greenmarket
bet. 17th St. / Union Sq. West

FOODS OF INDIA
Another Indian grocery.

121 Lexington Avenue
bet. 29th/30th Streets

HEALTH NUTS
Well-provisioned health food store.

835 2nd Avenue
bet. 44th/ 45th Streets

KALUSTYAN

123 Lexington Avenue
bet. 28th / 29th Streets

Well-stocked Indian Grocery. They feature bulk items such as raw pistachio nuts and sun-dried strawberries. .

PHILLIPS FARMS
:

Union Square Greenmarket
bet. 17th/ Union Sq. West

Peaches, Raspberries, Blueberries and Blackberries. March-December, M, Sa 8am-6pm.

RICK'S PICKS

Union Square Greenmarket
bet. 17th/ Union Sq. West

Rick, an Andover and Yale alum, quit his job as PBS producer to become a picklemeister.

Favorite pickle is Wasabean (green beans and wasabi). Wednesdays sunrise to sunset, year round.

GREENWICH VILLAGE

INTEGRAL YOGA NATURAL FOODS   229 West 13th Street
Health food shop   bet. Seventh/Eighth Avenues
Good quality and price on organics and bulk goods, plus hot and cold buffet. Some raw food dishes. Very popular.

LIFETHYME   410 Sixth Avenue
                                          at Eighth Street
One-stop shopping for large selection of exclusively organic produce, bulk goods, vitamins, herbal nostrums, and cruelty-free cosmetics. Amazing salad bar and delicious vegetarian food to go. Their vegan bakery turns out scrumptious pastries and prides itself on not using milk eggs or cheese in any of their cakes cookies or pies. They have a spiffy juice bar, and a good selection of books on nutrition and healing. Recently, they've added a living foods section with delicious raw pies, cakes and entrees.

STELLA McCARTNEY   429 West 14th Street
                                          bet. 9th/ 10th Avenues
The scion of Sir Paul sells vegan shoes and cruelty-free clothing of her own design.

EAST VILLAGE

COMMODITIES EAST   165 First Avenue
                                          at 10th Street
Health food shop with good quality and prices on organic produce and bulk goods.

4TH STREET FOOD COOP   58 East Fourth Street
                                          bet. Bowery and Second
All produce from leafy greens to tubers is organic, and the granola, grains, nuts and other bulk times are mostly so. Non-members are welcome.

HEALTHFULY OEGANIC MARKET   98 East Fourth Street
                                          bet. 1st / 2nd Avenues
Healthfully carries a full range of raw, vegan, gluten-free foods, organic products, and groceries as well as natural health and beauty aids. They specialize in raw, organic whole food vitamins; fully handcrafted organic herbal extracts ns supplements. They frequently have sales on premium health food products such as Zico Coconut water, etc.

HIGH VIBE HEALTH & HEALING 138 East Third Street (rear)
bet. 1st / A Avenues
A raw food superstore since '93 created by Bob Dagger, who has collected and created some of the largest selections of rawfood snacks, food, supplements, super foods, appliances, potions, books, beauty care, along with his nutritional counseling and classes; your one stop for everything you need for better health. A must visit also on line for great free recipes and free information: highvibe.com.

INDIA SPICE HOUSE 99 First Avenue
Indian grocery, 24 hours at 6th Street
Smaller than the Lexington stores, and the foodstuffs don't move so quickly, but still good— especially if you need some fenugreek or asafoetida in the middle of the night. 400 kinds of beer.

JIVAMUKTI YOGA CENTER 841 Broadway
bet. 13th/ 14th Streets
Yoga Center and emporium that sells yoga paraphernalia, eco-friendly clothing, books. It also features a new vegan cafe -cum-juice bar called JivamukTea, Try the Raw Lasagna, the Creator BLT, and chef Matthew Kenney's delicious raw desserts.

LIVE LIVE & ORGANIC 261 East 10th Street
bet. 1st Avenue / Avenue A
Raw foods boutique, featuring, a wide selection of books, super foods, snacks, potions, energizers and rejuvenatives. Also on sale are dehydrators, juicers and other accouterments of the raw food lifestyle. Consult their website: www.live-live.com

SUSTAINABLE NYC 139 Avenue A
bet. 9th/ 10th Streets
Local, organic, re-cycled, fair-trade, re-purposed, biodegradable, products and gifts.

WHOLEFOODS UNION SQUARE 40 East 14th Street
Organic supermarket. at Broadw

SOHO

BABY CAKES 240 Broome Street
Vegan baked goods. bet. Orchard/ Ludlow Streets

MAY WAH HEALTHY VEG. FOOD 213 Hester Street
bet. Centre / Baxter
Chinese Vegetarian grocery store. Well-stocked with mock meats such as mock shrimp, mock duck, mock squid, etc.

MOO SHOES   78 Orchard Street
                                                             bet. Grand/ Broome/ Streets
The best selection of cruelty-free shoes and accessories in the country.

OBSESSIVE COMPULSIVE COSMETICS
                                                             174 Lullow Street
                                                             bet. E. Houston / Stanton Streets
100% vegan cruelty free cosmetics and accessories in a stunning new bourtique.

WHOLEFOODS MARKET   95 East Houston Street
Organic supermarket.   at Bowery

BELOW CANAL STREET

WHOLEFOODS MARKET   270 Greenwich Street
Organic Supermarket

BROOKLYN

BACK TO THE LAND   142 Seventh Avenue
                                                             bet. Carroll Street/Garfield Place
Organically grown produce as well as grains, nuts and dried fruits are on offer. A wide range of
books, magazines and tapes are for sale. There is a section for homeopathic remedies. And a
well-stocked macro-biotic section.

CLEMENTINE BAKERY   299 Greene Street
Vegan baked goods   bet. Classon Avenue/Franklin St.

DOWNTOWN NATURAL MARKET   51 Willoughby Street
Organic produce, Juice and Salad bars.   off Jay Street

FAIRWAY   480-500 Van Brunt Street
The Manhattan food bazaar has come to Brooklyn.   Red Hook

FLATBUSH FOOD COOP   1318 Corydon Road
                                                             bet.Rugby and Argyle Rds.
Fresh organic produce. Earth-friendly household products. Open to non-members

PARK SLOPE FOOD COOP   782 Union Street
Members only organic market   bet. 6th & 7th Avenues

Members pay 20% above cost. Closed to Non-members.

PERELANDRA NATURAL FOOD CENTER   175 Ramsen Street
                                            at Court Street
Largest health food store in Brooklyn. Excellent juice bar and book section.

THE GARDEN   921 Manhattan Avenue
Well-stocked health food shop.   at Kent Street (Willaimsburg)

VAUTE COUTURE   234 Grand Street
                                            (Willaimsburg)
High fashion coats, printed dresses, overalls, etc, made from cotton, hemp, and re-cycled
materials. Founded and directed by Leanne Mai-ly Hilgart. *Vide* leanne@VauteCouture.com.

QUEENS

GNOSIS CHOCOLATE (raw vegan chocolate)   40-03 27th Street
                                              Long Island City
[Available at Westerly, High Vibe, Live Live & Organic, Jivamukti Yoga, & WholeFoods]

NEIL'S NATURAL MARKET   46-10 Hollis Court Avneue
                                              (Flushing)
Organic produce, vitamins, rawfooods, herbs, homeopathy, cruelty-free body care products, and
bulk items.

QUEENS HEALTH EMPORIUM   159-01 Horace Harding
Expy.Macrobiotic products, organic produce, juice bar.   (Flushing Meadows).

THE BRONX

GOOD 'N' NATURAL   2173 White Plains Road
Exceptionally well stocked Health Food Store (bet. Pelham Pkwy/Lydig Ave)

THEY CAN'T VOTE. *YOU CAN.*

NEW YORK LEAGUE OF HUMANE VOTERS

WWW.NYLHV.ORG

RAW FOOD RESOURCES

✿

New York has not only the greatest wealth of vegan and vegetarian restaurants in the world, it also has the greatest wealth of rawfood resources. If you count, Caravan of Dreams, , and the Westerley Raw Food Bar, New York now boasts fourteen raw food restaurants, and a growing number of raw food boutiques like High Vibe and Live Live, where the aspiring rawfooder may obtain nutritional guidance, instruction on raw food preparation, raw food snacks and useful gadgets like Food Processors, Saladacos (spiralizers). dehydrators, et al.

Restaurants

Caravan of Dreams
Partial raw menu

405 East 6th Street
bet. 1st/ A Avenues

Ginger Snaps Organic
Full raw menu

130 East 7th Street
bet. 1st/ A Avenues

Juice Press, The   at 14 locations:

JP 1
70 East 1st Street
bet. 1st / 2nd Avenues

Organic vegan raw juices, smoothies, and food
For other locations, consult neighborhood listings.

Organic Avenue   at 10 locations

116 Suffok Street
bet. Rivington/ Delancey Streets

Salads, raw dishes, and smoothies are prepared in the basement, and kept in a refrigerated display case on the ground floor. For other locations, consult neighborhood listings.

Pure Food and Wine
The ne plus ultra of raw food restaurants

54 Irving Place
bet. 17th/ 18th Streets

One Lucky Duck   at 2 locations
The take-out editon of Pure Food and Wine
See other location in Chelsea Market

125 1/2 East 17th Street
bet. 3rd Avenue / Irving Place

Quintessence
Mainly raw menu

263 East 10th Street
bet 1st / A Avenues

Rawlicious Full raw menu	249 Centre Street bet. Broome. Grand Streets
Rockin' Raw Full raw menu	171 Sullivan Street bet. Bleecker / Houston Streets
Squeeze, The Raw food truck	Union Square West
Westerly Raw Food Bar Raw food deli in NW corner of the store	911 Eighth Avenue at 54th Street

Raw Boutiques

Raw boutiques hold lectures, food prep classes; and sell super foods, raw snacks, books, gadgets, cosmetics, and other adjuncts of the vegan rawfood lifestyle.

HIGH VIBE 212-777-6645	138 East 3rd Street bet. First / A Avenues
LIVE LIVE & ORGANIC 212-505-5504	261 East 10th Street bet. 1st Avenue /Avenue A
ORGANIC AVENUE 212-334-4593	116 Suffok Street bet. Rivington/ Delancey Streets

Raw Vegan Chocolate

GNOSIS CHOCOLATE	Available at Westerly, High Vibe, Live Live & Organic, Jivamukti Yoga, et al.

Raw Potluck

HALLELUJAH ACRES POTLUCK 212-594-0718	Last Sunday 484 West 43rs Street Apt. 34k (Rev. Lawrence Rush)

Hands On Raw Food Preparation Classes

LIVE LIVE & ORGANIC   212-505-5504

ORGANIC AVENUE   212-334-4593

QUINTESSENCE   212- 501-9700

Raw Foods on the Internet

HIGH VIBE   www. highvibe. com

LIVE- LIVE & ORGANIC   www.live-live.com

LIVING FOODS INSTITUTE   www.livingfoodsinstitute.com

HALLELUJAH ACRES   www. hacres.com

FRESH NETWORK   www. fresh-network.com

RAW NUTRTIONAL COUNSELING,   www. doctorgraham.cc

Raw Resorts

Ann Wigmore Natural Health Institute, PO Box 429, Rincon, PR 00677; (787) 868-6307.

Aris La Tham's SunJoy Natural Life Retreat, Coyaba Springs, River Gardens & Falls, Shaw Park Ridge Estate, Ocho Rios, Jamaica (876) 441-0124, Sunfirefood@hotmail.com.

Vegan Living Foods Health Spa-Hippocrates Health Institute, 1441 Palmdale Court West Palm Breach, FL 33411; (407) 471-8876

Vegan Health Spa-The Regency Health Spa, 2000 South Ocean Avenue, Hallandale, FL 33009, (800) 454-0003

Water Fasting Center: True North, 4310 Lichau Road, Penngrove, CA 94951; (707) 792-2325

N ew York is the national capital of the publishing world, and is full of bookstores of all types—large chains carrying bestsellers, small dusty used bookshops, specialized technical or foreign-language stores. Here are some of our hangouts.

ALABASTER BOOKS..
Tel. 212- 982-3550
122 Fourth Avenue
at 12th

BOOKCOURT.. .....
Tel. 718-875-3677
363 Court Street
bet. Pacific/Dean

BOOKCULTURE.. ..
Tel. 212-865-1588
336 W. 112 Street
at Broadway

BLUESTOCKINGS..
Tel. 212-777-6028
172 Allen Street
bet. Stanton/Rivington Streets

CRAWFORD-DOYLE...
Tel. 212-288-6300
1082 Madison Avenue
at 82nd Street

KITCHEN ARTS & LETTERS............................
Tel. 212- 876-5550
1435 Lexington
at 94th Street

LOGOS BOOKS.................................. ....
Tel. 212-517-7292
1575 York Avenue
bet. 83rd/ *4th Streets

MERCER STREET BOOKS..................................
Tel. 212-505-8615
206 Mercer Street
at Bleecker Street

OPEN CENTER BOOKSTORE.............................
Tel. 212) 219-2527. Ext. 108
22 E 30th St
bet. Madison/ Fifth Avenues

QUEST BOOKSHOP...
Tel. 212- 758-5521
240 East 53rd Street
bet. Second/Third Avenues

SHAKESPEARE & CO.............................. ....
Tel. 212-529-1330
716 Broadway
at Waverly Place

ST. MARK'S BOOKSHOP...................................
Tel. 212-260-0443
31 Third Avenue
at 9th Street

SPOONBILL & SUGARTOWN..........................
718-387-7322
218 Bedford Avenue
bet. N. 4th / N. 5th Streets

STRAND...
Tel. 212-473-1452
828 Broadway
at 12th Street

THREE LIVES & CO...
Tel. 212- 741-2069
154 West 10th Street
at Waverly Place

USED BOOK CAFE...
Tel. 212-334-3324
120 Crosby Street
at Houston Street

Best Vegan Bites-2014

Best Appetizer: Jalapeno Hush Puppies @ Dirt Candy.

Best Salad: The Other Caesar @ Peacefood Café/Angel's Salad @ Caravan of Dreams.

Best Soup: The Pho @ Lan Café; Udon Noodle Soup @ Loving Hut.

Best Veggie Burger: The Jack Fruit Burger @ Bliss Grand; Eric's Jalapeno Daiya "Cheeseburger" @ Peacefood Union Square Café; Bean Burger @ Garden Café (Woodstock).

Best Sandwiches: Pan-Seared French Horn Mushrooms Panini @ Peacefood Café/ Vegan BLT @ The V-Spot: The Midtown Melt @ Blossom du Jour: The Autumnal @ Clementine Bakery

Best Sushi: The Spicy Mango roll at Beyond Sushi

Best Smoothie: Rain Forest Smoothie @ The Juice Press.

Best Entrée: Tofu and Roasted Kabocha Pumpkin in Sesame Soy Sauce @ Franchia/ Seitan Piccata @ Candle 79; Wild Rice & Cremini Risotto Croquettes @ Caravan of Dreams.,

Best Rice Dish: Bibenbap @ Franchia; Pineapple Fried Rice @ Wild Ginger

Best Noodles: Kim Chee Noodles, and Jap Chae Noodles @ Wild Ginger (Smith Street}.

Best Pizza: Mushroom Quxelle@ Peacefood Café.

Best Wrap: The Tempeh Wrap @ FoodSwings.

Best French Fries: French Fries @ FoodSwings.

Best Pastry: Danish Savory @ Clementine Bakery. Donuts,@ Dunwell

Best Dessert: Passionfruit "Cheese"cake @ Café Blossom (Carmine St.)

GLOSSARY

Baba ganoush	Middle Eastern spread made of eggplant, tahini, chick peas, lemon garlic.
Bagel	The classic New York bread. Chewy and sprinkled with onion, garlic, or seeds, and shaped like a donut. Eat one and you won't be hungry for hours. Usually vegan; ask about eggs and egg glaze.
Casein	A milk protein that accounts for cheese's ability to melt smoothly. Alas, it is added to nearly all soy cheese, making it unacceptable for vegans.
Chips	To an American, chips are crisps and fries are chips. Get it?
Dim Sum	Asian buffet: a selection of lots of different dumplings, savory cakes and the like.
Eggplant	Aubergine.
Falafel	The vegetarian meatball: a Middle Eastern deep fried patty of ground chick peas, garlic, and parsley.
Gluten	Chewy bland dough made from wheat flour which absorbs the flavors of the dish or sauce it's cooked in, like tofu. Common meat substitute.
Hummus	Middle Eastern spread made of ground chick peas, tahini, garlic, lemon and olive oil.
Knish	A savory pastry in which a simple thin dough is wrapped around a filling of potato, buckwheat, rice, etc. Usually vegan, but it pays to ask about cheese or butter, and whether the dough is made with egg.

I have from an early age abjured the use of meat, and the time will come when men such as I will look upon the murder of animals as they now look upon the murder of men.

LEONARDO DA VINCI, 1452-1519
Artist, scientist, inventor, engineer, architect
"Renaissance Man"

Kosher	Strict dietary guidelines followed by some Jews; they include a prohibition on mixing meat with milk in the same meal or the same kitchen. That means a kosher "dairy" restaurant will have no meat, with lots of options for ovo-lacto vegetarians but nothing for vegans, while a kosher restaurant that serves meat will have no dairy. Likewise, if a processed food is labeled "kosher," it won't contain both animal gelatin and milk powder, for instance.
Macrobiotic	A way of eating from Eastern traditions that seeks to bring foods into balance. Macro restaurants usually serve fish and sometimes eggs, but no dairy; they always have plenty for vegans.
Pico de Gallo	Mexican salsa made from raw onions, tomatoes, garlic, and cilantro.
Pretzel	On the street, these are big warm salty affairs that can stave off hunger in a pinch. They're 100% vegan.
Seitan	Gluten which has been boiled in a gingertamari broth.
Soy cheese	Soy milk processed to approximate the consistency and flavor of cheese. It almost always contains casein, a milk protein, so check to make sure it's vegan. (Soymage and Tofutti are typical brands of vegan cheese.)
Squash	A sweet autumn vegetable that comes in many types; pumpkin is one.
Tempeh	Fermented soybeans pressed into cakes, more flavorful than tofu.
Tempura	Vegetables dipped in batter and deep fried. Ask about eggs in the batter.
Tofu	Tofu is to soy milk as cheese is to cow's milk. Relatively bland, it soaks up the flavors of whatever it's cooked in.
Zucchini	Courgette.

CRUELTY-FREE SHOES

U ntil recently, it was scandalous that in New York, one of the world's great pedestrian cities, there were no shops that specialized in selling vegetarian shoes. But now with the advent of shops like Moo Shoes and 99X, you can buy non-leather shoes that are durable, breathable, and good-looking.

MOOSHOES

78 Orchard Street
bet. Grand/ Broome

Shoes, belts, and wallets all made by companies that make only leather-free goods.
www.mooshoes.com • 212-254-6512

PAYLESS SHOE SOURCE

9 NYC locations; check phone book

Inexpensive, leather-look plastic shoes that last about 6 months.

STELLA McCARTNEY

429 West 14th Street

Non-leather shoes, accessories and clothing.
www.stellamccarney.com • 212-255-1556

CRUELTY-FREE CLOTHING

STELLA McCARTNEY

429 West 14th Street

Non-leather shoes, accessories and clothing.
www.stellamccarney.com • 212-255-1556

VAUTE COUTURE

234 Grand Street
(Willaimsburg)

High fashion coats, printed dresses, overalls, etc, made from cotton, hemp, and re-cycled materials. Founded and directed by Leanne Mai-ly Hilgart. *Vide* leanne@VauteCouture.com.
www.vautecouture.com. • 347-422-0773.

WHY VEGANISM?

Vegetarians avoid meat because of the animal suffering, negative health effects, and environmental damage involved in "eating carcasses," as Leo Tolstoy put it. Vegans carry these reasons to their logical conclusion and avoid using all animal products, to the extent possible.

Cruelty

Milk and eggs are taken from animals kept in horrific conditions on factory farms. Hens are packed into cages so small they would peck each other to death if their beaks hadn't been cut off by a hot knife; these cages are jammed into buildings housing as many as 80,000 birds. After a few exhausting years of laying eggs over conveyor belts with fluorescent lights on 18 hours a day, spent hens are turned into soup. In cows, as in women, there is a connection between lactation and pregnancy: cows only give milk after giving birth. Therefore cows are artificially inseminated every year and their calves are taken away to be slaughtered for pet food or raised for veal in confining crates. Cows are injected with hormones to increase their milk output, tranquilizers to calm them down and antibiotics to keep them from succumbing to the diseases they contract from the unhealthy conditions in which they are kept. After five or six years of this treatment they are slaughtered. (The natural lifespan of a cow is 20 years.)

Health

Eggs are high in cholesterol, which contributes to heart disease, the leading killer in the United States. Milk products such as whole milk, cheese and yogurt are high in cholesterol and saturated fat, which has been linked to heart disease and cancer. Even non-fat milk products can be harmful: recent studies have linked milk consumption to cataracts and a diet high in animal protein to osteoporosis; while the Recommended Dietary Allowance of protein (for men) is 63 grams, vegetarian men consume an average of 103 grams. Intolerance of milk is the most common food allergy, leading to flatulence and respiratory and skin problems. The U.S. Department of Agriculture estimates that 50% of the dairy cattle in the herds along Mexico's northern border—whose milk is sold in the U.S.—are infected with tuberculosis. And everything the cow eats, from antibiotics to pesticide-laden grain, winds up in her milk. The American Medical Association states that a vegan diet provides all required nutrients, including calcium, iron, and vitamin B-12. Olympic gold medalist Carl Lewis is a vegan—need we say more?

Environment

Animals are kept in such concentrations in factory farms or feedlots that tons of their wastes, laden with pesticide and chemical residue, become a hazard. Livestock production accounts for a staggering 50 percent of America's fresh water use. The runoff from cleaning stalls is contaminated and pollutes acquifers and rivers. Eighty percent of the herbicides used in the U.S. are sprayed on soybeans and corn, most of which are fed to livestock. Livestock raising is the primary cause of topsoil erosion in the United States, but that doesn't stop the U.S. government from spending $13 billion on price supports for milk. 64 percent of U.S. agricultural land is used for livestock feed. Shouldn't we eat the grain and leave the cow's secretions for her calf?

FOR MORE INFORMATION

ANIMALS, HEALTH, AND THE ENVIRONMENT

Farm Animal Reform Movement,10101 Ashburton Lane, Bethesda, MD 20817; ((888) **FARM-USA**: www. FARMUSA.org

Farm Sanctuary-Organization for the Rescue and Protection of Farm Animals, PO Box 150, Watkins Glen, NY 14891; ☎ (607) 583-2225

United Poultry Concerns, PO Box 150, Machipongo, VA 23405-0150, ☎ (757) 678-7875

Society & Animals Forum, PO Box 1297. Washington Grove, MD. 20880-1297. ☎ (301) 963-4751

Animal People, PO Box 960. Clinton, Washington, 98236-0960, MD. 20880-1297, ☎ (360) 579-2505

People for the Ethical Treatment of Animals, 501 Front Street, Norfolk, VA 23510; ☎ (757) 622-PETA

Friends of Animals 1841 Broadway, #812 , New York, NY 10023, ☎ (212) 247-8120

Animal Legal Defense Fund, 127 Fourth Street, Petaluma, CA 94952, ☎ (707) 769-7771

North American Vegetarian Society, PO Box 72, Dolgeville, NY 13329, ☎ (518) 568-7970

New York League of Humane Voters, 151 First Avenue, Suite 237, New York, NY 10009. ☎/ 212-889-0303; www.nylhv.org

American Vegan Society, 56 Dinshah Lane, PO Box 360, Malaga, NJ 08328, ☎ (856) 694-2887

Institute for Integrative Nutrition, 3 East 28th Street, 12th floor, NYC, NY 10016☎ (212) 730-5433. Offers natural cooking classes with no animal products.

Institute for Food and Health and The Natural Gourmet School, 48 West 21st St., 2nd Floor, ☎ (212) 645-5170. Natural cooking classes and a Friday night vegan feast.

Woodstock Farm Animal Sanctuary, Woodstock Sanctuary. Org., ☎ (845) 679-5955.

VEGAN DELIGHTS

Vegan Catering in NYC; The Regal Vegan. www.regalvegan.com. ☎(732) FAUX-GRAS.

Vegan Chocolate Decadence, ☎ (800) 324-5018

Vegan Dried Fruits-Rainforest Delights, ☎ (626) 284-8001

Vegan Parmesan, Parma, ☎ (541) 665-0346

Vegan Organic Produce Home Delivery Service-Urban Organic, ☎ (415) 412-1336

Vegan Organic Cookies and Brownies-Allison's Gourmet, ☎ (800) 361-8292

✉ FEEDBACK ✉

Please write to let us know how we can improve the next edition of The Vegan Guide to New York City. Tell us about new restaurants, changes, closings, great meals, whatever you like.

_____

_____

_____

_____

_____

Your address: _____

_____

_____

_____

Additional copies.

For additional copies of The Vegan Guide to New York City,
send $9.95 plus $3.00 postage each to:

Rynn Berry, 159 Eastern Parkway,
Suite 2H, Brooklyn, NY 11238.
tele/fax: (718) 622-8002.
Email: berrynn@att.net.
Web: vegsource.com/berry.
www. veganguidetonyc.com

ALSO AVAILABLE: Rynn Berry's other bestselling books:
• *Famous Vegetarians* and *Their Favorite Recipes* @ $16.95 plus $3.00 postage.
• *Food for the Gods: Vegetarianism and the World's Religions* @ $19.95 plus $3.00 postage.
• *Hitler: Neither Vegetarian Nor Animal Lover* @ $10.95 plus $3.00 postage.
•*The New Vegetarians* @ $10.95 plus $3.00 postage
• *Becoming Raw* @ $24.95 plus $3.00 postage.

For copies of:
The Vegan Passport @ $5.00;Vegetarian London @ $10.00;
Vegetarian Britain @ $13.50; Vegetarian France @ $12.00;
Vegetarian Europe @ $13.50; send the designated amount, plus $3.00 postage, to Attention: Freya Dinshah, The American Vegan Society, 56 Dinshah Lane, PO Box 360, Malaga, NJ 08328 USA.

Notes

Notes

Notes

Notes

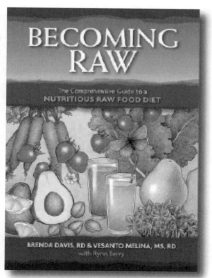

**plants
for
hunger**

Feed Families & Save Animals

Plants-4-Hunger is an animal-friendly gift-giving campaign (for you or from you).

We send 100% of your gift to these 4 vegan programs:

1. Soy protein in school-lunch program - Belize
2. Community farming and water projects - India, Kenya and Brazil
3. Urban vegetable farming benefiting soup kitchen - USA/Michigan
4. Weekly feeding program for homeless adults & children - Ethiopia

Please visit **www.awfw.org/gifts** to find out more and donate online.

Text **AWFW** to **55678** to stay connected via mobile.*

www.AWFW.org

awell-fedworld
feeding families / saving animals

815 Otis Place, NW, Washington, DC 20010   202.495.1348   care@awfw.org

*Message & data rates apply. Max 3msgs/month. Text STOP to end.